StrictlyG

THE GOLF BALL HANDBOOK, REVISED EDITION

Written by Louis G. Caschera, Jr.

ISBN 0-9644781-1-0

Published by: StrictlyGolf, Inc.
882 Eckford
Troy, MI 48098
248-926-6169
Fax 248-926-6170

www.StrictlyGolf.com

Strictly Golf™ BALLS

THE GOLF BALL HANDBOOK, REVISED EDITION

Written by Louis G. Caschera, Jr.

For those who enjoy the game of golf

ISBN 0-9644781-1-0

www.StrictlyGolf.com

Preface

Welcome to the second edition of "Strictly Golf BALLS, The Golf Ball Handbook." The first edition was such an overwhelming success, *thanks to you*, that we've decided it was time to update the golfer about the new and ever-changing golf ball technology being constantly introduced to us by the industry's manufacturers.

Since the publishing of our first edition, which by the way was and is the only comprehensive book on the market dedicated to golf balls and its technology, we've received a tremendous amount of feedback from our readers and even the manufacturers. This feedback included everything from, "I didn't know that," to thanking us for educating them, helping them find the right golf ball and improving their game.

Interestingly enough, and as we expected, we also received feedback from several golf ball manufacturers stating their differences and opinions about the results from the independent golf ball testing we did. Most were satisfied with the results, and some were not. Oh well, that's why we did the independent study and test -- to make sure you're getting the real scoop on a ball's performance so you can be your own judge.

During our ongoing research about the types of golf balls on the market, we've found that most tend not to have a marketing life cycle beyond 2 years. Since the last publication of *Strictly Golf BALLS*, almost all of the golf balls on the market at that time have either been replaced or improved. Like golf clubs, manufacturers are always looking for ways to introduce the better ball for us. The technology changes we see from an existing golf ball to its "new and improved" release varies -- and that is what we point out in this new edition of *Strictly Golf BALLS*. *As a bonus, we also included a brand new section containing published results of an independent*

1

study and test we did against the most popular drivers on the market today. We'll not only tell you what golf ball goes the farthest when hit at different swing speeds, but what *driver* hits them the farthest!

We are very proud of this new edition of *StrictlyGolf BALLS*. We have committed and dedicated ourselves to you as a comprehensive source for unbiased advice and information about golf products, services, and consumer concerns. A very important ingredient to our existence includes our independent studies and testing of golf products and services so that we can keep you informed. So turn the pages and enjoy -- and don't forget, your feedback is very important to us and always welcomed. Please drop us a line.

Contents

Introduction

StrictlyGolf™ BALLS
The Golf Ball Handbook, Revised Edition

Have you ever notice the little attention and lack of knowledge given to a golf ball's technology as you wandered through your favorite pro shop? What about the lack of information on golf ball performance and comparison as you flip through the pages of a golf magazine?

It seems like the only information on a golf ball these days is usually found in the form of an ad with claims that their ball goes farther and straighter than their competition's. Or claims about how the new wangle-tangle technology and materials like titanium, double covers, and teardrop dimples are better than ever. Like golf clubs, manufacturers are always looking for ways to introduce and market the better golf ball to us. As a result, there are even more types and brands of golf balls on the shelves these days than ever before. And we thought choosing a personal computer for ourselves with all the right memory, disk size, speeds and feeds and software was difficult!

In recent years, significant advances and refinements have taken place in golf ball technology from cover to core. Not only are manufacturers developing golf balls for every style of play, they're now taking advantage of the excitement generated in the club business with *titanium*. Can you believe it? They're now making golf balls with titanium!

Instead of getting clearer, the ball market has become more confusing than ever for the consumer. For example, we now have a two-piece ball being called a three-piece ball because it has a *double-cover* covering the core!

More significantly, ball makers are now concentrating more and more on making golf balls which conform to different types of playing styles and characteristics. This includes designing and making golf balls specifically to perform optimally with the best-selling drivers in the business! Before we know it even club manufacturers, such as Callaway, will be getting into the business of designing and making golf balls which perform best when used with their own clubs!

Because of these technology advancements, there's a greater need to educate the golfer about how these changes can affect their game. We also need to dispel any belief that the golf ball is unimportant or of little importance.

Recent studies have revealed that every golf ball demonstrates its own pattern of behavior toward a golfer's wide range of abilities and individual swing characteristics.

Take a moment and turn to the contents of this publication and look at the list of golf balls which are available on the market today. There are balls made specifically for all levels of players - from the pro's on down to the average player, including seniors and ladies. For the consumer, the ball market of today has become so confusing that it has left them in a quandary about which ball to buy and use.

The average golfer will purchase two to five new dozen golf balls a year. While some will be able to hang on to most of them for a season, others typically play the more experienced ball found while looking for the one he or she hit off the fairway. A high percentage of balls purchased are subjected to the hazards lining the fairways only to be found and re-cycled by someone in a foursome behind you or by the professional golf ball seeker who makes a living selling them back to you.

The average golf ball of today is selling for around two dollars and rising. Compare that to the petty cost of our clubs, or our shoes, or even the cost of joining a fancy country club and the golf attire we wear. And yet you and I will probably go through four dozen of balls a year - and so will all the 20 million or so regular golfers. That's an awful lot of money being spent on that little white ball, and the manufacturers know it. They want our attention badly and will develop the marketing hype to get it.

To gain the publics eye on being the maker of the golf ball that the professionals play, the golf ball manufacturers are battling each other through marketing savvy more than anything else these days. Of course you and I can buy the same type of ball that the pros play at our local pro shop - and whether a Titleist or Maxfli is really better than a rock is beside the point thanks to the canny marketing that "their ball is for the better players."

A few golf ball manufacturers, such as Top-Flite, Titleist, and Maxfli, have done a excellent job at marketing their products as the best and what the pros hit -- and they certainly priced their product accordingly. What this created for other golf ball manufacturers was a leftover market to fight over -- a market addressing the millions of hackers who destroy and lose balls by the billions each summer. As a result, we're now seeing other golf ball makers coming to market with claims that their balls fly farther, straighter, feel softer, have multi-layer covers, a titanium core, and even patented dimples. Marketing has blurred the boundary between image and reality! Well read on, because we're about to clear up that boundary.

So, to help you wade through all of this golf ball marketing hype, **StrictlyGolf BALLS, The Golf Ball Handbook**, a handy and comprehensive guide, was developed and recently updated. It has valuable information, not found anywhere else, about all types of golf balls from the various golf ball manufacturers. Not only will you find information about the balls as advertised by their manufacturers, you will find information not told by the manufacturers. *You will find the results of an independent study we did comparing each ball's performance characteristics.*

We put each ball against the same set of testing parameters - and these parameters are more realistically in line with today's golfer (i.e., a robot hitting each ball with a club speed of 80, 90 and 100 mph).

We've also included a SPECIAL BONUS for you in this revised edition. A brand new section is included with published results of an independent study and test we did against the most popular DISTANCE DRIVERS on the market today.

Now you can find out not only what golf ball goes the farthest when hit at different swing speeds, but what driver hits them the farthest and most accurate!

StrictlyGolf BALLS, The Golf Ball Handbook is a must for every golfer. It is intended to help the golfer gain knowledge about the golf ball and about the balls on the market today. Use this information to compare some of the basic construction fundamentals and performance characteristics about each golf ball and determine what type of golf ball might best suit you and the type of game you play. This handy guide will provide you with a consistent starting point as indicated in the results of our independent golf ball tests.

A very important point to keep in mind when choosing a golf ball to fit your game is your golfing ability and swing characteristics. This all translates into consistency. Consistency is what is needed to get any golf ball to perform the same way each time. If there is any deviation in your swing, your club speed, and all other elements of hitting a golf ball, then there is a change in consistency - and thus a change in the performance of the golf ball. There is no single golf ball that optimizes all the performance benefits of control, distance and feel. So when you study a manufacturer's statistics about their golf ball, keep this in mind. Your goal should be to find a golf ball that fits you and your consistencies or one that is as forgiving to your inconsistencies.

So, when you need to know who are all the manufacturers of a three-piece ball with a balata or a surlyn cover that have a high trajectory flight pattern with a high spin rate - you can find it here in **StrictlyGolf BALLS, The Golf Ball Handbook.**

Golf Ball Evolution

No single element has had greater influence on golf's development than the golf ball itself. The nature and effectiveness of the various types of balls have shaped the way the game has evolved and greatly influenced the way golf clubs are designed today.

The game of golf has changed dramatically over the years and so has the evolution of the golf ball. There were six notable stages in the evolution of the golf ball with the first being the feathery ball during the 1400's.

1400 - The Featheries

The first golf ball was a leather sack stuffed with goose feathers. The leather sack was stitched together and then soaked before being filled with wet feathers. When drying, the feathers would expand while the leather contracted which resulted in a very hard mass that was then hammered into roundness and sometimes painted white. There is recorded evidence that the feathery performed notably well. It wasn't uncommon to get drives of 300 or more yards.

1860 - Gutta Percha

This was the first rubber like golf ball which was made from a type of tree sap which was hard but yet resilient in its natural state. By heating the sap, it became soft enough to be hand shaped into a one-piece ball. It was more durable than the feathery ball but did not offer the same distance.

1870-80 - Hand-Hammered Gutta

It was discovered that a ball's flight was notably longer and more accurate after it had been nicked through use. With this discovery, ball manufacturers started to provide balls that had a gutta percha cover with an even pattern of nicks that were hand hammered into it.

1890 - Bramble

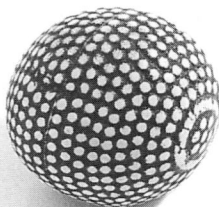

The discovery of the hand-hammered gutta led to the use of molds made of iron and ball presses which would create consistent surface textures and patterns. During this time, the most popular pattern was the bramble which were raised round bumps in a pattern of concentric circles.

1900 - Wound Rubber Ball

The wound rubber ball was considered a major breakthrough in the game of golf. It consisted of rubber thread that was tightly wound around a solid rubber core with a gutta percha cover. Although this ball lacked uniformity of size and weight, golfers had a ball with a livelier core and were able to control the spin more.

1930 to present - Modern Ball

The modern ball today is more consistent because it follows the USGA specifications for size, weight, velocity, driver distance and symmetry. With this, the golfer now gets a more consistent and variety of golf ball performance to suit the individuals game. More playable golf balls continue to be designed with newer technological advancements in materials and manufacturing processes.

The Legal Golf Ball

There are five United States Golf Association (USGA) specifications which all golf balls must conform to under controlled conditions: **size**, **weight**, **velocity**, **driver distance**, and **symmetry**.

USGA Golf Ball Specifications	
Size	The golf ball cannot be smaller than 1.68" in diameter. There is no maximum. A smaller ball can actually fly farther due to decreased drag. Oversize balls are perfectly legal and are typically designed to reduce hooks and slices because of an overall lower spin rate.
Weight	No more than 1.62 ounces. There is no minimum. A heavier ball can actually fly farther due to increased momentum; on the other hand, lighter balls may be easier for slow swingers to get airborne.
Velocity	This is also referred to as ball speed (not club speed). It is how fast the ball goes when you hit it. The golf ball cannot exceed more than 250 feet/second in an atmosphere of 75°F when tested on a USGA machine. A maximum tolerance of 2% is allowed or 255 feet/second.
Distance	*The maximum distance of a golf ball when tested on a USGA driving machine with a club speed of 160 feet/second, shall not exceed 280 yards total, plus a tolerance of 6% or 296.8 yards. The club speed at 160 feet/second translates to approximately 109.09 mph.
Spherical Symmetry	A golf ball shall not be designed to perform differently when hit from various sides of the ball. The non-slice golf ball from a few years ago didn't pass the spherical test.

* While manufacturers design golf balls which closely approach this driver distance specification, there is no upper limit for how far a player can drive a ball which is dictated by the club speed.

Worldwide, golf balls which conform with USGA rules can weigh no more than 1.62 ounces (45.9 grams). In most countries, golf balls must measure at least 1.68 inches (4.27 centimeters) in diameter. The British golf ball is slightly smaller - 1.62 inches (4.11 centimeters) in diameter - and was the standard in Great Britain for many years and is still used in some competitions.

There are some golf balls being manufactured today which are slightly larger than 1.68" but yet meet the weight requirements and match the maximum legal initial velocity of 250 feet per second.

A question often asked today is whether or not most golf balls are the same. Golf balls of today are being designed to meet a combination of performance characteristics such as higher spin rates, softer feel, high or low flight trajectories, cover durability, and distance. To meet such playing characteristics, golf balls are being made with different combinations of core and cover materials as well as several types of dimple designs for the aerodynamics of the ball. Because of this, *golf balls are not the same*. Usually, the initial velocity and overall distance are the USGA-limits which most golf balls reach when tested Other hidden factors which can affect golf ball performance is a poor manufacturing quality assurance process. If a golf ball manufacturer has quality assurance problems, then all USGA limits may be impacted.

The Modern Day Golf Ball Design

A golf ball that is properly designed and manufactured uses the laws of physics to help enhance a golfers performance. The golf ball and its construction technology has been and is becoming more important as a critical element in the game of golf. Even titanium is playing a role these days in golf ball construction. Some of the new balls feature a powdered mixture of these metals as part of the core or cover compounds. The theory is that the added metal enhances the strength of the compounds and modifies the weight distribution.

Golf balls of today are being designed to meet playing characteristics such as spin rate, feel, trajectory, durability, and distance. In order to meet these playing characteristics, golf balls are being manufactured with a combination of different covers, cores and dimple designs.

A golfer's role in ball performance is actually relinquished once the ball leaves the face of the golf club. Up to this point, you and your golf club have provided the initial velocity and angle of the golf balls' departure. It is now the forces of natural law, particularly the aerodynamics, that take over.

Manufacturers are designing and constructing balls to take advantage of two forces that a golf ball will encounter; club impact and the flight of the ball. At impact, the ball compresses against the club and the frictional force between the club head and the ball puts a backward spin on the ball as it springs into its flight. During impact, the construction of the ball's cover, core, and compression play a very important role in its performance toward the initial velocity and distance. When a ball is in flight, the dimples on the ball play a very important role in distance and symmetry because the dimple design and layout have the ability to create turbulence which adds to the lift and carry of the ball.

Covers

Golf ball covers primarily affect the feel, spin and durability of a golf ball. Balata, surlyn, zylin, and elastomer are some of the proven cover materials being used today. But beware. The golf ball manufacturers are continuously looking for ways to improve covers (and sometimes confuse the consumer) with the latest and greatest materials. As a matter of fact, cover technology is one of the fastest changing areas in golf ball technology. An example of this ever changing technology is the use of *titanium* in cover materials. Why not? They got us all excited about titanium in clubs. There's claims being made that titanium in a cover strengthens the chemical bond between materials which creates more resiliency and, in turn, more distance. Well, see for yourself in the section "Independent Test Results" of this book and you be the judge.

The thickness and the hardness of the cover on a golf ball varies. Usually, the softer the cover, the longer the ball will stay on the club face when hit, resulting in more spin and better feel. This is more noticeable on short iron shots because the cover deforms into the club's grooves causing the ball to roll up the club face and spin more. A harder cover will tend to slide (instead of roll) up the club face which causes less spin.

For the most part, the average golfer who decides what cover to choose comes down to pure economics. Many of today's golfers have turned to durable covered balls simply because they know that an occasional mis-hit won't scuff or cut the cover.

Cover Hardness

Cover hardness is one of the many determining factors toward helping you pick a golf ball to meet your style of play. Most above average golfers prefer a softer covered ball because it allows them to control it better than a hard covered ball when hit off their irons. So you may ask, how is the hardness of a cover determined? By knowing what the *"Shore D"* rating is. The term "Shore D" is a rating (and process) being used by some manufacturers to measure the hardness of the cover. Cover hardness can be measured with an instrument called a Durometer. Shore, just so happens to be a brand of a Durometer. The Durometer is a small gauge with a needle that is depressed into the cover. The gauge reads how hard or soft the cover material is. The results are reported as a number; the lower the number, the softer the material.

Double Cover/Multi-layer

You may have heard the term *"double cover"* or *"multi-layer"* being used by some of the golf ball manufacturers. These terms typically apply to the construction type of two-piece balls. This is a design in which the large core of a two-piece golf ball is covered by a harder inner layer (about the same thickness of the cover), which is then covered by a soft or hard cover. The performance concept behind the inner layer of a "double cover" or "multi-layer" ball is to provide a combination of feel and distance. The intention of the additional cover is to give you low spin rates off the driver and high spin rates on short iron shots. See section "Multi-layer Golf Balls" for a better understanding of this new technology.

Balata Cover

A balata cover is a type of natural rubber made from a synthetic source that is chemically and physically equivalent to natural balata. Balata is the softest of all other covers. A balata covered ball will spin easier and is preferred by players who demand maximum feel and control. This means more control over shots where the action of the ball is critical.

Surlyn Cover

Surlyn is a trade name for a group of thermoplastic resins developed by the Dupont Corporation. It was the first and most durable cover material to revolutionize the construction of a golf ball when introduced 20 years ago. Surlyn, or similar material blends are what most golf ball manufacturers use today to produce durable covers. A durable cover offers better cut and abrasion resistance than a balata cover. Surlyn covered balls generally feel harder than balata covered balls. The hardness of this cover material accounts for a lower spin rate.

Inside the Golf Ball

The source of energy in a golf ball is its *core*. It provides the essential components for the ball's maximum initial velocity off the club face. Its construction type is what affects the spin rate (control), velocity (distance) and compression (feel). The primary core constructions of a golf ball is either wound or solid.

A wound core is a small solid or liquid filled rubber ball that is wound with rubber thread. A solid wound center is simply a small, solid rubber ball. The liquid wound center is a small, hollow rubber ball which is filled with either a liquid or a paste. With both types, the centers are wound to a predetermined size to optimize velocity and spin and then either a balata or durable cover is applied. The amount of thread used per golf ball varies. Usually, about 35 yards of thread will be stretched to about 275 yards as it is wound. A wound core construction is also referred to as a *three-piece ball*.

A solid core with a cover is referred too as a two-piece ball. The core is composed of a single piece of solid, elastic material and is typically made of a high resiliency rubber compound with a blend of additives to further enhance its performance. A cover is then applied.

But beware here too. Again, the golf ball manufacturers are continuously looking for ways to improve the performance of the core by introducing new blends and formulas. A *titanium* core? They say it works in clubs, so why not in the core of a golf ball. There's claims being made that using titanium in a core acts to bond all the materials in the core into a single cohesive unit. This bonding action allows all of the energy from the club to be transferred in the same direction at impact. In contrast, a standard core is not bonded, and the energy is randomly dispersed at impact. Well, why don't you be the judge on this. See for yourself in the section "Independent Test Results" of this book.

Two-Piece Golf Balls

Initially, two-piece golf balls were used by most of the average everyday golfers because it combined durability with maximum distance. Consisting of a large core and a relatively thin cover, two-piece balls were traditionally categorized as distance balls because of their lower spin, higher velocity and harder feel. Today, the two-piece golf ball is being used by many professionals thanks to the improved core and cover technologies. As a result of these new technologies, you can now get a two-piece ball with performance characteristics that are similar to that of a three-piece ball. The performance characteristics of two-piece balls that are available on the market include combinations of distance, durability, feel and spin.

A common construction of the two-piece ball includes a single solid core, usually made of a high resiliency rubber compound with a blend of additives to further enhance its performance, which is then enclosed in the ball's cover.

For the two-piece ball that is being built for distance, the solid core is typically a high-energy acrylate or resin and is covered by a durable, cut-proof cover which gives the two-piece ball more distance than any other ball. These "hard" balls are covered in either surlyn, a specialty plastic proprietary to the Du Pont company, or a similar kind of material. The two-piece is virtually indestructible and with its high roll distance, it is by far the most popular golf ball among ordinary golfers. Typically it is harder to control because of its lower spin rate.

Multi-Layer Golf Balls

Another technology enhancement is the *"double cover"* or *"multi-layer"* two-piece golf ball. These terms typically apply to the construction type of two-piece balls but are also used in some new three-piece balls. This is a design in which the large core of a two-piece golf ball is covered by a harder inner layer (about the same thickness of the cover), which is then covered by a soft or hard cover. The performance concept behind the inner layer of a "double cover" or "multi-layer" ball is to provide a combination of feel and distance. The cores are designed for driver distance, the inner layers are customized for full iron shots, and the cover type can offer ultimate feel and spin in half shots, chips and putts.

The intention of the additional cover is to give you low spin rates off the driver and high spin rates on short iron shots. What manufacturers are telling us is that the relative hardness between layers enables them to tailor the spin characteristics of the ball. Given that, they can make it a high-spinning ball or a low-spinning ball. Does this mean just like clubs, they can now make custom fitting golf balls?

To help you understand this a bit more, let's review what happens when a club comes in contact with the ball. When you hit a ball with a driver, you have a higher-impact velocity, meaning the ball leaves the club face faster than one hit with a short-iron or wedge. There are two reasons why this happens, you have a faster swing speed and less loft. As you go from your driver down to your wedge, the compression on the ball at impact decreases with each club. The harder you hit it, the deeper the compression of the ball. The deeper the compression, the more the core comes into play.

Now according to the manufacturers of these double-covered golf balls, the inner cover helps reduce the compression at impact so that the ball jumps off the club face faster and with less spin when hit with a driver. On the other hand, when the ball is hit with a wedge, the compression is not as severe and that allows for the softer, outer cover to pinch against the club face causing the ball to spin more.

Three-Piece Golf Balls

Three-piece golf balls or wound balls have either a solid rubber or liquid center core which is covered by many yards of elastic windings, over which is molded a cover of durable surlyn, surlyn like, elastomer, or balata. With both types of cores, the centers are wound to a predetermined size to optimize velocity and spin and then either a balata or durable cover is applied. The amount of elastic winding used per golf ball varies. Usually, about 35 yards of elastic winding will be stretched to about 275 yards as it is wound.

Wound balls are softer and take more spin, allowing skillful golfers more control over the ball's flight when hit. It typically has a higher spin rate than that of a two-piece ball and is more controllable by good players. A surlyn cover is a thermoplastic resin that is harder than a balata and is considerably more durable; it is virtually uncuttable. A balata-covered, liquid-centered, three-piece ball takes longer to manufacturer than a two-piece ball. The wound construction over a liquid center, combined with a soft synthetic balata cover, produces a very high spin rate, providing maximum control and feel.

Manufacturing a Golf Ball

During golf's first modern day boom which was from the turn of the century until the depression, manufacturers made balls with all kinds of interesting core materials: rubber, gum, cork, and steel. Today, golf balls can be lumped into two construction categories: two-piece or three-piece golf balls.

Most three-piece ball manufacturers follow the similar process of first freezing the liquid and solid cores so that they remain round during the winding process. The winding equipment used automatically wraps rubber thread around each core to the required thickness, and at the same time maintains a precise wrapping pattern and tightness of winding. The compression factor of a three-piece golf ball was largely determined by the tightness of winding. Today, each ball is wound to a predetermined size to optimize velocity and spin. The size of the thread, length, tension and pattern of the windings determines the velocity of the ball's core.

The solid core of a two-piece ball which contains a high resiliency rubber compound with a blend of additives to further enhance its performance is mixed and then molded into spheres. In final core finishing, every core is ground with a centerless grinding machine to give a uniform core size, weight, velocity and compression for consistent performance.

The next step is to put a cover around the core. There are two methods of installing a cover that are typically used by the manufacturer - compression molding or injection molding.

For compression molding, the covers are initially molded in half shells which are then assembled around the core and molded together and the dimples are pressed into the cover material. This cover construction is sometimes referred to as a two-piece cover. This type of method is not generally used today.

With injection molding, a mold cavity is used in which the core is placed and held in the cavity with pins. The molten cover material is injected into the cavity that surrounds the core. As it cools and hardens, the pins retract and the molded ball is ejected from the mold. This cover construction is also referred to as a one-piece cover.

From this point on, the process is essentially a cosmetic one. A Surlyn cover's color can be created by blending the Surlyn pellets with color pigments before processing begins. Balata covers require painting. The ball is then stamped and clear coated.

Markings on a Golf Ball

All golf balls which conform to the USGA specifications have identification markings on the ball. Each marking on a golf ball is either categorized as a major or minor marking which usually identifies the make and type of the ball.

Major markings on a golf ball are referred to as pole markings. They are typically represented by the larger print identifying the title of the ball. For example, ULTRA 500 will be found stamped on the ball in two locations - referred to as the pole locations of the ball. The pole locations are equally spaced from each other, just as the north and south pole markings on our planet earth.

A minor marking is also referred to as the seam marking (even though most covers are constructed without seams these days). This marking is usually represented by smaller print on the golf ball. Using the same ULTRA 500 golf ball as an example, WILSON-90 would be found stamped on the ball between the two pole markings.

Players commonly use these markings as a reference point when striking the golf ball. It allows them to always position the ball in the same and consistent manner prior to teeing it off or putting it.

Other markings on a golf ball are the black or red numbers. *Typically*, these numbers relate to the compression rating of the golf ball; a black number for a 100 compression ball; a red number for a 90 compression ball. For a clearer understanding of what golf ball compression is really about, read on.

Compression - Myth or Fact

Compression is probably the most misunderstood measurement in golf ball design. Many people have no idea or the wrong idea of what compression is and what it means.

In the early days of golf, the term compression was originally used as a measurement for golf ball quality. It was actually used to reference the tightness of the windings around the center core of a three-piece ball - the tighter the windings the better the ball performed. This created a long-standing perception that compression affects golf ball distance and performance.

Because golf ball technology uses newer heat-resistant threads with newer and better winding equipment for three-piece balls, golf ball compression has become merely a condition of feel. And now with the availability of the consistent quality of a two-piece ball, compression as a measurement of quality is just about obsolete.

Today, the word "compression" in the golf ball industry relates to a value expressed by a number in the range from 0 to 200 that is given to a golf ball. This number defines the deflection that a golf ball undergoes when subjected to a compressive load. Compression simply measures how much the shape of a golf ball changes under a constant weight.

As golf balls come off the production line, all three-piece balls and some two-piece balls are measured for compression and rated. A standard weight is applied to each ball - one that doesn't compress is rated 200; a ball that deflects 2/10ths of an inch or more is rated zero. Between those two extremes, for every 1/1000ths of an inch that the ball compresses, it drops one point from 200 and the compression rating is then established.

Most balls have compression ratings of either 80, 90 or 100; the lower the compression, the softer the feel. Not every ball marked 80, 90 or 100 is exactly that rating. The actual rating can fall roughly within 3-5 points on either side of 80, 90 or 100. Any balls that fall out of this range are usually discarded, sold as range balls, or sold as second quality balls (X-OUTs).

There have been several published tests to prove that golf ball compression relates more to feel and your own superstition than its performance. The conclusions were, if you take different rated golf balls (i.e., 100, 90, or 80 compression) which have the same construction, aerodynamics and cover material, and use an automatic golf swing machine such as the Iron Man, the yardage difference between the balls hit were negligible, less than two yards.

Aerodynamics of a Golf Ball

The science of aerodynamics and its affect on golf ball performance have golf ball scientists spending more research time than ever in this frontier. They are determined to design that one ball that will soar through the air like a flying machine.

The fact is, these scientists have found out that air has a lot to do with the trajectory of a flying golf ball. And they're proving it. Tests have been conducted in which a golf ball that flies 225 yards in a normal atmosphere would only fly about 150 yards in a vacuum. Like airplanes with wings, if there is no air, they can't fly. In a normal atmosphere, the spinning ball causes lift and suspends itself against gravity thus flying farther even though it is meeting wind resistance (or drag). If the air weren't there, the ball couldn't sustain its lift and there would be no drag.

The flight of a golf balls is actually a wondrous display. The amount of hang time it gets is amazing. How does it do this? It's all possible with controlling a combination of a few aerodynamic forces -- lift and drag.

Lift and Drag

An airplane wing causes lift by angling the position of the wing into the wind. By angling the front of the wing up, the air is deflected downward thus causing an upward force, or *lift*. A similar reaction can occur with a golf ball believe it or not. If a golf ball were placed in an airstream head on with no movement (i.e., no spin), disturbance would occur but no lift. But give it a little back spin and guess what happens, it creates lift! Like the airplane wing deflecting the wind downward, a spinning golf ball also causes the wind to deflect downward and creating lift.

With any object moving through the air, you'll get some drag. But with a ball flying through the air, you'll get a lot of drag. The reason for this, it's a ball trying to cut through the air and not an airstreamed designed wing. To reduce the drag on a golf ball, it was found that dimples actually reduce the air wake and cause the flow of air to travel farther around the ball before separating. Thus, a dimpled golf ball has only half the drag than that of a smooth one.

So, what do we have. We have a golf ball which will soar through the air because the spinning causes more lift while the dimples reduce the drag.

Dimple Geometry

Let's first review the purpose of dimples. When a golf ball is in flight, its dimples manipulate the air flow around it thus affecting its flight. Dimples assist in removing the resistance from the front of the ball to the rear. The primary function of dimples is to sustain the ball's initial velocity as deep into its flight as possible by displacing the air uniformly to produce longer spin times and reduce the drag. Different shapes, sizes, their depth, and the patterns of the dimples all affect the ball's flight differently.

Golf ball manufacturers have spent millions of dollars in trying to convince us that their dimple design is the perfect design that perfects the right combination of dimple sizes, shapes and patterns. Granted, the placement of dimples on a golf ball is crucial to its distance and control, but there is no one perfect dimple.

Most golf balls today have anywhere from 300 to 500 dimples. It is becoming more evident that the number of dimples on a golf ball is becoming a less important factor in a ball's flight performance. If this weren't true, manufacturers would be providing us with golf balls with thousands of dimples on them.

What is required though, is that dimples should cover a golf ball's surface as much as possible. If dimples cover about 65% or less of the surface, then there appears to be a significant decrease in the carry distance of a golf ball. In today's golf balls, most dimple patterns are taking up approximately 85% of the ball's surface.

Typically, there are five basic patterns which are used and can be laid around a sphere - OCTAHEDRON, DODECAHEDRON, TETRAHEDRON, CUBE, and an ICOSAHEDRON. Usually, the pattern used by a golf ball manufacturer tries to maximize the number of repeating geometric elements. They do this because aerodynamic consistency is a function of the symmetry of the surface design. The theory is that when the dimples are precisely placed within each repeating element on the ball, the ball spins the patterns against the encountered air, thus the resisting air is exactly the same and the result is non-disrupted air flow.

The Effects of Large, Shallow Dimples

Air Flow

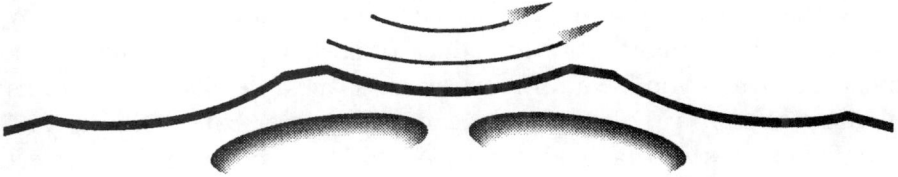

With large shallow dimples, the air will move quickly over and through the dimple. This reduces drag significantly but increases lift disproportionately. The results could produce a higher trajectory with a greater raw distance potential. If there is any draw back to this it would be the loss of control because of the high trajectory.

The Effects of Small, Deep Dimples

Air Flow

With small, deep dimples, air is caught in the dimples (like a puddle) which forces the ball down. This does not reduce the drag as much as the large dimple but it does tend to decrease the lift. The results typically produce a low trajectory which could minimize the distance as well as a short carry.

The Effects of a Combination of Dimple Sizes

It was found that dimples actually reduce the drag of a golf ball while in flight. They reduce the air wake and cause the flow of air to travel farther around the ball before separating. Thus, a dimpled golf ball has only half the drag than that of a smooth one. Dimples help sustain the ball's initial velocity as deep into its flight as possible by displacing the air uniformly to reduce drag and produce longer spin times. So, when you have different sizes, shapes, depths, and patterns of dimples on a golf ball, it can affect the ball's flight, and manufacturers try to take advantage of this by producing that perfect ball that gives in-flight stability no matter what.

The Key to Accuracy

The key to accuracy starts with your swing. At the point of contact with your club face and ball, your swing generates the ball's velocity, launch angle and the ball's spin rate. Ball velocity is how fast your ball goes when you hit it. The launch angle is the angle the ball leaves your club face. Spin rate is how fast the ball spins when it leaves the club face. This combination -- velocity, launch angle and spin rate -- produces the type of distance you will achieve. If all is perfect up to this point and you've launched the ball from the sweet spot on your driver, your shot should be straight and long.

Let's talk about ball velocity for a moment. Ball velocity is not the same as clubhead speed. Clubhead speed is how fast you swing your club. You produce your ball velocity with clubhead speed. As you will see in our test results of the independent testing, ball velocity is always faster than your clubhead speed. Typically, a pro will generate a ball velocity of 160 mph with his driver. Your average day-to-day male golfer will generate a ball velocity of 130 mph with his driver. If you're looking for distance, and since ball velocity is generated by the swing you have, you may want to look for a club that has lighter material with a large clubhead, and a high velocity golf ball.

As for spin rate, we've already mentioned that this is the amount of spin (or rotation) a golf ball has when it leaves your club face. There are times that your swing type may have a negative impact on the spin rate -- causing that awful hook or slice. There are golf balls on the market which can help reduce these hooks and slices. Balls with a low spin rate construction will help minimize your hooks and slices.

The launch angle is the angle the ball leaves your club face. At this point the aerodynamics of a golf ball takes over along with the initial direction, spin rate and speed of the ball.

We all know that aerodynamic forces affect the motion of objects. Like aircraft manufacturers, the manufacturers of golf balls use the principles of aerodynamics in designing their golf balls. When a golf ball takes flight, it penetrates the air and there is resistance. When a golf ball is in flight, the dimples help diminish this resistance by manipulating the air, removing the resistance from in front of the ball and turbulently displacing it to the rear. But different dimple designs do this differently.

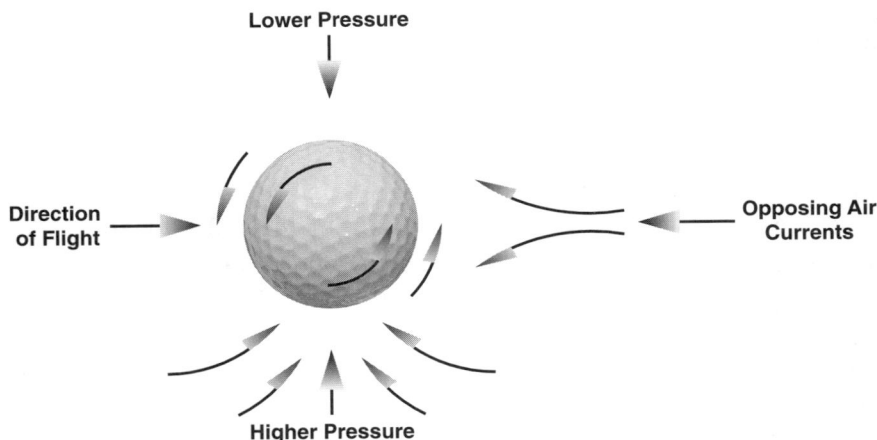

A well hit golf shot is hit into the air with backspin. As the ball spins counter clockwise, the dimples grip the opposing air and spin it around the ball. Since greater air pressure builds below the ball than above, the ball rises to the area of least pressure resistance.

The principle that manufacturers use behind dimple design and golf ball compression (the feel of the ball, the hardness or softness of the ball) is one that produces a golf ball which provides in-flight efficiency and accuracy. It is uniform air-flow that allows the golf ball to rivet to its flight path. By sustaining a consistent spin velocity on the ball, off line slippage (hooking or slicing) can be reduced. This is true for both two-piece and three-piece constructed ball types.

Flight Path - A Two-Piece Distance Ball

A ball that **compresses less** on the club face (a harder feeling ball and most two-piece distance balls) will slide up the club face on impact giving it a higher launching angle. This will cause a lower spin rate on the ball because of less deflection and stored energy. As a result, the trajectory flattens (less spin), you will get less carry and more roll. Typically, a two-piece ball will not slip sideways as much as a wound ball.

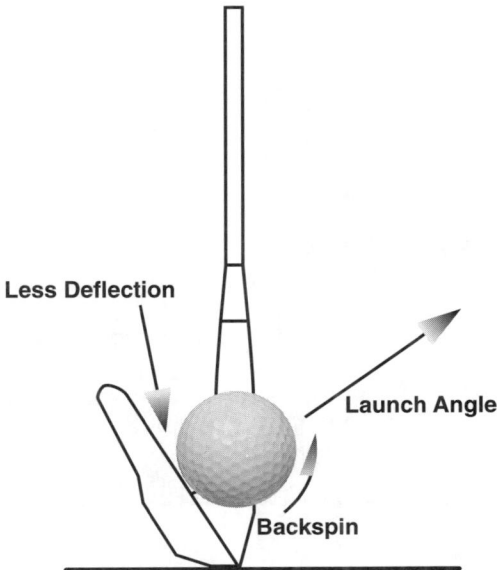

Flight Path - A Three-Piece Ball

A ball that **compresses more** on the club face (a softer feeling ball and most thread-wound balls) will resist sliding up the club face thus storing higher torsional energy for launch. Because the ball resists sliding up the club face at impact, a lower launch angle is created (over most two-piece balls) with a higher spin rate. As a result, you get more lift with a higher trajectory. A thread-wound ball will tend to move (slip) off-line more than a two-piece ball.

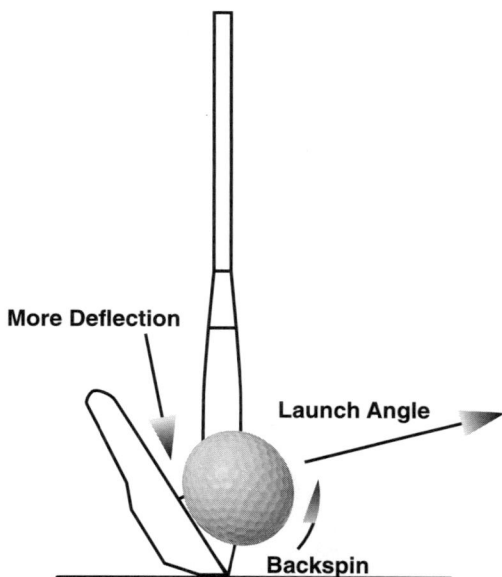

More Deflection

Launch Angle

Backspin

Differences Between Golf Balls

Visually, the difference in the various brands of golf balls offered in the pro shops today is very small. This real difference is found mainly in the construction type from cover to core.

To help you understand these differences while you search for your golf ball that is just right for you, keep the following construction characteristics of a golf ball in mind while comparing one manufacturer's golf ball to another.

O The Construction Type

A golf ball's construction is either called a two-piece, multi-layer or three-piece ball. A three-piece ball consists of a small core that is wound with a rubber band and then covered with either a balata or durable cover. It is typically softer and provides a higher spin rate for better control. If you can control the ball around the greens, a three-piece ball is best for you. If you're interested in distance alone, stick with a two-piece distance ball. A two-piece ball consists of a large core which is covered by either a balata like or durable cover. Once you learn to start controlling the ball (i.e., fade, draw or spin the ball), look into the higher performance two-piece balls. Also, make sure you check to see if the ball conforms to USGA specifications. If so, it is considered a legal golf ball which can be used in PGA tournaments.

O The Cover

A golf ball's cover is either a balata, balata like, surlyn, surlyn like, or another durable material blend. The thickness or thinness of a cover varies from one type of ball to another and is directly related to how the ball feels when you strike it. The cover material also affects a ball's spin rate. You might also pay attention to the type of markings are on the ball. Check if there are proper markings on the ball which represent the poles and seams. Also note if the number on the ball is printed in black or red which usually represents the balls compression rating.

○ The Dimples

Dimples on a golf ball manipulate the air flow around the ball while in flight. When choosing a golf ball, note how many dimples there are, their size, what type of pattern they are in, and their shape. Check the dimple's size, shape and depth. Are they small or large, or is it a combination of both. Are the dimples deep or shallow. Remember, the primary purpose of dimples are to help reduce the drag and sustain the golf ball's initial velocity while in flight. When a golf ball manufacturer offers different trajectory types (high or low) of the same ball, it is usually the dimple pattern which differentiates them.

○ The Core

The core is the center construction of a golf ball. When looking into a three-piece ball, check if the core is a wound liquid center core or a wound solid center core. When looking into a two-piece ball, determine how the core is constructed by the manufacturer (type of material) and its performance claims. By doing this, it will help you determine the type of performance you can expect from the ball (i.e., a distance ball, a ball with feel, or a softer ball with a high spin rating, etc.).

Choosing a golf ball to suit your game is a matter of tradeoffs. The construction type, cover, dimples and the core of a golf ball all affect its performance. When choosing the right ball for you, you need to find the balance between performance characteristics, style of play, equipment and weather.

Caring for Your Golf Balls

A golf ball's performance can change depending on the type of care it's given during its play time, storage time and weather.

The best way to store your golf balls is to keep them in a cool, dry, dark place. Room temperature is fine, but around 50°F is best. In the summer, don't leave your golf balls in the trunk of your car. In the sun, the temperature in the trunk can reach 150°F - which is hot enough to change the shape.

If properly stored, a balata ball is good for at least two to three years. Two-piece balls can last up to five years. Even when properly stored, balls change with age. Wound balls will loose compression over time, while the core of a two-piece ball gets harder with age and gains compression. In fact, a core of a two-piece ball could crack with age.

A slight scuff or smudge won't noticeably affect a ball's performance. However, a bad scuff or smile will change the way a ball flies - it may not travel as far and it might wobble, take a sudden dive or get knocked down in the wind more quickly than normal. If your ball has gone out of round it should be discarded.

Hot weather can cause a three-piece ball to lose compression, so try a higher compression ball to compensate. A two-piece ball may also feel a little softer in the heat, but some companies say this actually means an extra yard or two.

When the temperature drops, there's also a drop in the initial velocity of the ball off the club head - a three-piece ball dropping about twice as fast as a two-piece ball. A balata cover also feels harder in the cold. So you might want to try a two-piece over a three-piece ball in cold weather (around 40° to 50°F).

We haven't tested what effect exposing golf balls to water has on their performance. Some manufacturers are saying that on average, after one week , a two-piece ball loses six yards off a drive. A three-piece ball is worse. You'll have to wait until the next edition when we'll include performance testing of water soaked golf balls.

Specs at a Glance

This section contains information about the most current and popular golf balls on the market today. It is intended to give you enough general information about each golf ball's features so you can compare and decide which ball may best fit your game at a glance.

Each listing will contain information about a ball's construction and performance characteristics as advertised by its manufacturer.

The average price for a dozen of golf balls varies by several dollars depending on the pro shop you frequent. Most discount stores will sell golf balls for far less than the suggested manufacturers retail price. I would highly recommend calling around to get prices of the golf balls you're interested in.

Golf Ball Listing

On the following pages, to help you quickly identify the construction type of the ball (i.e., two-piece or three-piece balls), look for one of the following icons to be displayed next to each ball listed. All balls listed conform to the USGA specifications.

Two-Piece

Multi-Layer

Three-Piece

Example of Listing Information

The following is an example of the golf ball listing and what information can be found for each ball.

NAME OF GOLF BALL, compression

 or  or

Manufacturer: Company who manufacturers the ball

Construction: Either a Two-Piece, Multi-Layer or Three-Piece ball

Cover: Surlyn, Surlyn blend, Balata, or Balata like

Ball Size: 1.68" (Standard ball size) or 1.72" (Oversize)

Core: Solid, Wound Solid Center, Wound Liquid Center

Spin Rate: rpm's when hit with a driver and/or iron

Dimples: Total number of dimples on the ball and its pattern

Competition: Other Balls that Compare to this one

Performance Characteristics: General performance characteristics of the golf ball.

Acushnet Company

Pinnacle Gold LS 90, 100

Manufacturer: Acushnet Company
Construction: Two-Piece
Cover: Lithium Surlyn
Ball Size: 1.68"
Core: Solid Polybutadiene
Dimples: 392/Icosahedron

Performance Characteristics: The Longer and Straighter (LS) ball. A ball that is designed for distance, and durability. For golfers who want to reduce hooks and slices without sacrificing distance. Very soft feel due to new core technology. Its dimple pattern promotes a slightly higher trajectory for distance and softer landing on the green.

Pinnacle Gold 90, 100

Manufacturer: Acushnet Company
Construction: Two-Piece
Cover: Lithium Surlyn
Ball Size: 1.68"
Core: Solid
Dimples: 392/Icosahedron

Performance Characteristics: The new and improved feel. Its dimple pattern promotes a slightly higher trajectory for distance and softer landing on the green.

Pinnacle Distance Extreme

Manufacturer: Acushnet Company
Construction: Two-Piece
Cover: Lithium Surlyn
Ball Size: 1.68"
Core: Solid Polybutadiene Type
Dimples: 392

Performance Characteristics: A ball that is designed for golfers who demand the maximum distance allowed by the rules of golf. Produces maximum initial velocity.

Provides low, boring trajectory for maximum roll and overall distance. Contains a high energy core.

Pinnacle Distance Oversized

Manufacturer: Acushnet Company
Construction: Two-Piece
Cover: Lithium Surlyn
Ball Size: 1.72"
Core: Solid Polybutadiene Type
Dimples: 392

Performance Characteristics: Designed for golfers who want to maximize their distance with straighter flight. Benefits include maximum initial velocity, reduces hooks and slices, sits up high; easier to hit. An oversized design with a high energy cover and low spin construction.

Pinnacle Equalizer

Manufacturer: Acushnet Company
Construction: Two-Piece
Cover: Lithium Surlyn
Ball Size: 1.68"
Core: Solid Polybutadiene Type
Dimples: 392

Performance Characteristics: Designed for golfers who typically hit their drives less than 200 yards and want to maximize their distance potential. Benefits include increased distance without having to over-swing, and optimized ball flight for increased distance. A high lift construction ball with a high energy core giving high, distance trajectory.

Pinnacle For Women

Manufacturer: Acushnet Company
Construction: Two-Piece
Cover: Surlyn
Ball Size: 1.68"
Core: Solid Polybutadiene Type
Dimples: 392

Performance Characteristics: Designed for women golfers who want a distance ball with a softer feel. It has a softer compression core and a soft surlyn cover.

Titleist and Foot-Joy Worldwide

New Titleist Professional 90, 100

Manufacturer:	Titleist Company
Construction:	Three-Piece
Cover:	Elastomer
Ball Size:	1.68"
Core:	Wound Liquid Center
Dimples:	392/Icosahedron

Performance Characteristics: The new Titleist Professional golf ball utilizes the Tour proven wound technology, an exclusive Elastomer cover and a new advanced thermoplastic liquid filled center to deliver performance, distance and durability for Tour players, as well as mid to low handicap golfers. The new Professional delivers a wind-piercing trajectory for added distance, with soft feel, control, accuracy and consistency from tee to green.

Titleist HP2 Tour

Manufacturer:	Titleist Company
Construction:	Two-Piece
Cover:	VLMI and Lithium Surlyn, .05" thick
Ball Size:	1.68"
Core:	Solid, Common Polybutadiene (PBD)
Dimples:	440/Modified Cuboctahedron

Performance Characteristics: Features balata like feel and superior distance for golfers seeking optimum spin, improved control and workability. The thinner, advanced soft surlyn cover combines with an oversized core to deliver tremendous feel and shot-making precision.

Titleist HP2 Distance

Manufacturer:	Titleist Company
Construction:	Two-Piece
Cover:	High Resilience and Lithium Surlyn
Ball Size:	1.68"
Core:	Solid, Common Polybutadiene (PBD)
Dimples:	440/Modified Cuboctahedron

Performance Characteristics: The HP2 Distance is made for golfers seeking superior distance with enhanced, softer feel. The oversized core combines with a cut-proof surlyn cover to deliver higher initial velocity and exceptional distance, carry and roll.

Titleist Tour Balata 90, 100

Manufacturer:	Titleist Company
Construction:	Three-Piece, liquid center, wound core
Cover:	Balata, .040" thick
Ball Size:	1.68"
Core:	Wound Liquid Center, 1.125" diameter
Spin Rate:	Driver - 4100 rpm, 8 iron - 9000 rpm
Dimples:	392/Icosahedron

Performance Characteristics: A ball that provides control and workability because of its soft feel and spin. It has a liquid center, wound core and balata cover that resists scuffing. If you are looking for more feel and control than distance, this ball will provide you that. The liquid center results in a more penetrating trajectory, particularly in the wind. Titleist has a patented winding process and dimple design that helps balance the lift and drag of the ball.

Titleist Tour Distance 90, 100

Manufacturer:	Titleist Company
Construction:	Three-Piece, liquid center, wound core
Cover:	Ionomer
Ball Size:	1.68"
Core:	Wound liquid filled rubber center
Dimples:	392/Icosahedron

Performance Characteristics: The new Titleist Tour Distance features advanced liquid-filled center wound technology and a new responsive high performance ionomer cover to provide golfers with exceptional spin, soft feel and maximum distance. Reduced driver spin rate producing a flatter ball flight for longer carry and roll distance. Significantly lower compression for exceptionally soft feel.

Titleist DT 80, 90, 100

Manufacturer:	Titleist Company
Construction:	Three-Piece, wound core
Cover:	HFM Surlyn, .080" thick
Ball Size:	1.68"
Core:	Wound Solid Center, 1.56" dia
Dimples:	392/Icosahedron

Performance Characteristics: For the golfer seeking soft feel, superior distance and cut-proof durability. It features advanced wound technology and a new, resilient cut-proof cover which results in longer, straighter distance while retaining the wound ball feel. Lower initial winding tension, faster velocity and a lower spin rate contributes to the new DT Wound's increased distance.

Titleist DT-2 Piece

Manufacturer:	Titleist Company
Construction:	Two-Piece
Cover:	HFM Surlyn, .050" thick
Ball Size:	1.68"
Core:	Solid, Common Polybutadiene
Spin Rate:	Driver - 3050 rpm, 8 iron - 7550 rpm
Dimples:	392/Icosahedron

Performance Characteristics: The DT 2-Piece features advanced solid construction and a new resilient cut-proof cover to deliver longer distance off the driver and irons. It achieves maximum distance with soft feel. The newly formulated cut-proof cover complements the high energy core and dual dimple icosahedron aerodynamics.

Ben Hogan Company

Hogan 428 Extra Distance 90, 100

Manufacturer:	Ben Hogan Company
Construction:	Two-Piece
Cover:	Zinc, Lithium, Sodium Surlyn
Ball Size:	1.68"
Core:	Solid, Polybutadiene
Spin Rate:	Driver - 3100 rpm, 8 iron - 7900 rpm
Dimples:	428/Tetrakaidecahedron

Performance Characteristics: This two-piece distance ball features a thinner cut-proof cover over a large core. It's dimple pattern provides optimum trajectory and carry. This ball flies as far as the Rules of Golf allow and it produces a mid-spin which reduces hooks and slices.

Hogan 428 Pro 90, 100

Manufacturer:	Ben Hogan Company
Construction:	Two-Piece
Cover:	Soft VLMI Surlyn, .07" thick
Ball Size:	1.68"
Core:	Solid, Polybutadiene
Spin Rate:	Driver - 3100 rpm, 8 iron 8800 rpm
Dimples:	428/Tetrakaidecahedron

Performance Characteristics: This two-piece ball is Hogan's extra spin ball. It's softer cover is designed to resist scuffing and cutting while providing for better spin control and a green grabbing bite. It's dimple design is for optimum trajectory and carry. It's has a high energy core designed for distance.

Hogan 428 Extra Control 90, 100

Manufacturer:	Ben Hogan Company
Construction:	Three-Piece
Cover:	Zinc, Lithium, Sodium Surlyn
Ball Size:	1.68"
Core:	Wound Solid Center
Spin Rate:	Driver - 2600 rpm, 8 iron - 8500 rpm
Dimples:	428/Tekrakaidecahedron

Performance Characteristics: The Hogan three-piece constructed 428 ball is designed for extra control and features a high speed thread for providing more distance. This ball is designed to produce wound ball control and feel for maneuverability with a cut-proof cover.

Bridgestone Sports (USA), Inc.

Precept Dynawing Double Cover

Manufacturer:	Bridgestone Sports (USA), Inc.
Construction:	Two-Piece Double-Cover
Cover:	Surlyn
Second Layer:	Optimum Transformation Cover
Ball Size:	1.68"
Core:	Solid
Dimples:	392/Octahedron

Performance Characteristics: Designed for the golfer whose first priority is distance with feel. Its double-cover construction allows for stronger shots at any clubhead speed, yet offers golfers the feel of a soft, wound ball. The aerodynamic cover design also creates a higher trajectory, enabling golfers to stop their approach shots more easily.

Precept Tour Double Cover

Manufacturer:	Bridgestone Sports (USA), Inc.
Construction:	Three-Piece Double-Cover
Cover:	Surlyn
Second Layer:	High Repulsion cover
Ball Size:	1.68"
Core:	Wound Solid Center
Dimples:	395/Hexagonal

Performance Characteristics: Designed for the golfer who is seeking the highest levels of spin and feel. It combines all of the characteristics of a wound balata ball with added distance and durability. Is referred to as a four-piece ball. It's aerodynamic hexagonal dimple design produces a more boring trajectory into the wind for more distance. It has two covers, then a wound layer around a inner solid core.

51

Precept EV Extra Spin

Manufacturer: Bridgestone Sports (USA), Inc.
Construction: Two-Piece
Cover: Surlyn
Ball Size: 1.68"
Core: Solid
Dimples: 392

Performance Characteristics: For golfers looking for additional control without sacrificing distance. Offers high spin for approach shots, but lower spin rates off the driver and long irons for exceptional distance. It provides the feel and control similar to that of wound balata golf balls, while maintaining the distance and consistent flight path of a two-piece ball. The ultra-high velocity core and unique 392 double-dimples provide ideal flight trajectory and consistent performance in virtually all playing conditions.

Precept EV Extra Distance

Manufacturer: Bridgestone Sports (USA), Inc.
Construction: Two-Piece
Cover: Surlyn
Ball Size: 1.68"
Core: Solid
Dimples: 432 cone dimples

Performance Characteristics: For golfers looking for a ball that pushes the USGA distance standards to the outer limits, but performs exceptionally around the green. Its dynamic core generates more velocity than any other ball in the Precept EV line. It's gradational core technology minimizes side spin for more accurate shots. An aerodynamic cover produces a boring mid-trajectory flight for exceptional performance especially in windy conditions.

Precept EV Lady

Manufacturer: Bridgestone Sports (USA), Inc.
Construction: Two-Piece
Cover: Surlyn
Ball Size: 1.68"
Core: Solid
Dimples: 432/quasicosahedral

Performance Characteristics: This ball is engineered for the majority of women who find the traditional two-piece ball far to firm. It combines a super soft high velocity gradational core and blended surlyn cover for maximum performance at clubhead speeds of 80 mph or less. It's designed to provide lower spin rates, resulting in less side spin for longer, straighter shots. A resilient cover makes the ball extremely durable, while its dimple pattern produces a mid-trajectory flight for optimal distance with less dispersion.

Precept EV Senior

Manufacturer:	Bridgestone Sports (USA), Inc.
Construction:	Two-Piece
Cover:	Surlyn
Ball Size:	1.68"
Core:	Solid
Dimples:	432/quasicosahedral

Performance Characteristics: Developed for more moderate swing speeds, the Precept EV Senior's high velocity core generates exceptional distance without sacrificing a soft feel for playability around the green. It incorporates the same two-piece technology found in the Extra Spin ball, producing minimal spin rates off the driver for more accurate shots. Its durable, cut resistant cover makes the mid-trajectory senior ball that can be depended on for numerous rounds.

Precept MC Distance

Manufacturer:	Bridgestone Sports (USA), Inc.
Construction:	Two-Piece
Cover:	Surlyn like
Ball Size:	1.68"
Core:	Solid
Dimples:	392

Performance Characteristics: Precepts longest and softest two-piece ball. It provides distance, extraordinary feel and high spin rates never before found in the two-piece distance category. It incorporates a new muscle-fiber core technology which in concept is similar to the fibers of a human muscle. Linking agents within the core bond the rubber molecules stronger and more closely together than in traditional two-piece balls. This results in maximum conservation of energy for improved distance and exceptionally soft feel. The ultra thin DS (distance-spin) cover allows golfers better feel and more spin. The thinner cover also plays a role in making the muscle-fiber core larger and more powerful than previous designs.

Cayman Golf Company

Grand Tour II 100

Manufacturer: Cayman Golf Company
Construction: Two-Piece
Cover: Titanium Surlyn
Ball Size: 1.68"
Core: Solid

Performance Characteristics: A two-piece 100 compression, titanium-surlyn cover golf ball for maximum distance. Cayman ranks this ball as a very long ball. Designed for the high-mid handicap player.

Grand Tour III 90

Manufacturer: Cayman Golf Company
Construction: Two-Piece
Cover: Ionomer
Ball Size: 1.68"
Core: Solid

Performance Characteristics: A two-piece 90 compression, ionomer covered ball. A soft cover. Cayman compares this ball with the Titleist DT 90. Designed for the mid-low handicap player.

Grand Tour IV

Manufacturer: Cayman Golf Company
Construction: Three-Piece Double Cover
Cover: Surlyn
Ball Size: 1.68"
Core: Solid

Performance Characteristics: Cayman calls this their four-piece double cover ball. It provides the golfer with feel and distance and is considered more durable than the Top-Flite Strata. Optimum trajectory with outstanding feel. Designed for the low-professional player

Grand Tour Balata 100

Manufacturer: Cayman Golf Company
Construction: Three-Piece
Cover: Urethane-Balata
Ball Size: 1.68"
Core: Solid

Performance Characteristics: A three-piece 100 compression golf ball. It contains a urethane-balata cover and is Caymans highest spinning ball. Designed for the low handicap player.

David Geoffrey & Associates

Slazenger 420p Power-Control

Manufacturer: David Geoffrey & Associates
Construction: Two-Piece
Cover: Surlyn
Ball Size: 1.68"
Core: Solid
Dimples: 420/modified Icosahedron

Performance Characteristics: A ball for the more aggressive player willing to challenge the course with powerful impact speed and the confidence to fire at the flags. A new dimple pattern along with a new, larger high-response core produces riveting trajectories while a new cover formulation keeps all this energy under tight control with optimum spin rates. Very long with plenty of action.

Slazenger 420d Raw-Distance

Manufacturer: David Geoffrey & Associates
Construction: Two-Piece
Cover: Surlyn
Ball Size: 1.68"
Core: Solid
Dimples: 420/modified Icosadodecahedron

Performance Characteristics: A ball designed for the player wanting to squeeze every yard out of every shot but not at the sacrifice of in-flight stability. The combination of large dimples (for length) and small dimples (for control) along with new cover and core construction technology produces amazing on-line distance. Expect a crisp feel, instantaneous velocity, and breakthrough distance.

Slazenger 420t Tour-Calibre

Manufacturer:	David Geoffrey & Associates
Construction:	Two-Piece
Cover:	Surlyn
Ball Size:	1.68"
Core:	Solid
Dimples:	420/modified Octahedron

Performance Characteristics: A ball designed for the shot-making player who manages the game and works the course, generating distance as needed and finesse as wanted. New dimples combined with a thin, more pliable cover and softer, larger core produce satisfying length enhanced by the feel, touch, spin and maneuverability which demanding professionals and low-handicappers seek.

Dunlop Golf Division

Shark Attack Life Spin

Manufacturer:	Dunlop Golf Division
Construction:	Two-Piece
Cover:	Soft Surlyn
Ball Size:	1.68"
Core:	Solid
Dimples:	432

Performance Characteristics: A high spin two-piece ball that gives you feel, spin and control to attach the toughest pin placements. It features the distinctive Greg Norman logo.

Shark Attack Distance

Manufacturer:	Dunlop Golf Division
Construction:	Two-Piece
Cover:	Surlyn
Ball Size:	1.68"
Core:	Solid
Dimples:	432

Performance Characteristics: A powerful distance two-piece ball featuring a high velocity core and durable cover. If features the distinctive Greg Norman logo.

DDH Explosive Distance 110

Manufacturer:	Dunlop Golf Division
Construction:	Two-Piece
Cover:	Surlyn
Ball Size:	1.68"
Core:	Solid
Dimples:	360/Dodecahedron

Performance Characteristics: The first DDH 110 compression ball on the market. A ball engineered with a high energy solid polybutadiene core for optimum carry and roll for every kind of swing. You get longer wood and iron shots. A durable cut proof cover. Designed for players who are seeking distance and straighter shots. It has a wind resistant dimple pattern for in-flight stability.

DDH Explosive Distance + Control

Manufacturer:	Dunlop Golf Division
Construction:	Two-Piece
Cover:	Surlyn
Ball Size:	1.68"
Core:	Solid
Dimples:	360/Dodecahedron

Performance Characteristics: This ball reduces side spin for straighter shots. Offers the distance of the 110 in a 90 compression ball that delivers distance with a lower, straighter flight path. The core is a high energy, spin reducing polybutadiene with a surlyn cover for lower trajectory and in-flight stability.

DDH Explosive Distance + Spin

Manufacturer:	Dunlop Golf Division
Construction:	Two-Piece
Cover:	Surlyn
Ball Size:	1.68"
Core:	Solid
Dimples:	360/Dodecahedron

Performance Characteristics: This ball is designed for high, soft approach shots. Offers the great, high spin performance of a three-piece ball with the distance of a two-piece ball. A softer core produces a high initial velocity for distance with a significantly softer feel. A durable surlyn cover that generates optimum spin for approach shots.

DDH Explosive Distance for Women

Manufacturer:	Dunlop Golf Division
Construction:	Two-Piece
Cover:	Surlyn
Ball Size:	1.68"
Core:	Solid
Dimples:	360/Dodecahedron

Performance Characteristics: The Explosive Distance for Women is a lower compression distance ball designed for the female golfer. The lightweight core boosts lift and distance and the dimple pattern provides optimal trajectory, improved roll and enhanced in-flight stability.

Maxfli Revolution 90, 100

Manufacturer:	Dunlop Golf Division
Construction:	Two-Piece Double Cover
Cover:	Urethane surlyn like
Ball Size:	1.68"
Core:	Solid

Performance Characteristics: The Revolution is Maxfli's new multi-layer ball, which is long off the tee and soft on approach. Unlike some of the other companies making multi-layer balls, Maxfli makes its mark my changing the softness of the inner, not the outer, cover, so feel doesn't come at the expense of distance. It has a large, solid core covered with a thin layer of elastic. On top of this is a urethane cover.

Maxfli XS Tour

Manufacturer:	Dunlop Golf Division
Construction:	Two-Piece
Cover:	Surlyn Type
Ball Size:	1.68"
Core:	Solid

Performance Characteristics: The Maxfli XS Tour is a newer ball designed for accuracy. Exceptional Spin, feel and control. For the player who wants maximum spin and control without sacrificing distance. A two-piece ball with a scuff-resistant surlyn cover and a high-spin core.

Maxfli XS Distance

Manufacturer:	Dunlop Golf Division
Construction:	Two-Piece
Cover:	Surlyn Type
Ball Size:	1.68"
Core:	Solid

Performance Characteristics: The Maxfli XS Distance is a newer ball designed for distance accuracy. Has a softer feel.

Maxfli MD Tungsten

Manufacturer:	Dunlop Golf Division
Construction:	Two-Piece
Cover:	Surlyn Type
Ball Size:	1.68"
Core:	Solid

Performance Characteristics: The Maxfli MD Tungsten is a newer ball designed for distance, distance, distance. The Maxfli MD Tungsten mixes tungsten oxide metal with the rubber core to produce distance. An optimum trajectory ball designed for distance and stability in windy conditions. Has a softer feel. Designed for players who desire maximum distance from a 2-piece ball.

Maxfli XF 90, 100

Manufacturer:	Dunlop Golf Division
Construction:	Three-Piece
Cover:	Durable Balata
Ball Size:	1.68"
Core:	Wound Solid Center
Dimples:	432/Icosadodecahedron

Performance Characteristics: The Maxfli Exceptional Feel ball. For the player who wants the ultimate in spin, feel and control with enhanced durability. The feel and control of balata, with a more durable cover, The Maxfli XF's three-piece construction duplicates the playability of the original Maxfli HT Balata.

Maxfli MD 90, 100

Manufacturer:	Dunlop Golf Division
Construction:	Two-Piece
Cover:	Durable Lithium Blend
Ball Size:	1.68"
Core:	Solid
Dimples:	432/Icosadodecahedron

Performance Characteristics: An optimum trajectory ball designed for distance and stability in windy conditions. Has a softer feel. Designed for players who desire maximum distance from a 2-piece ball.

Maxfli HT Balata 90, 100

Manufacturer:	Dunlop Golf Division
Construction:	Three-Piece
Cover:	Balata (urethane)
Ball Size:	1.68"
Core:	Wound Liquid Center
Dimples:	432/Icosadodecahedron

Performance Characteristics: The premier balata ball by Maxfli. For the player who wants the ultimate in feel, spin, control, and tournament performance. A scuff-resistant balata cover. This three-piece, liquid center and balata covered ball provides optimum feel and performance.

Maxfli XS 90, 100

Manufacturer:	Dunlop Golf Division
Construction:	Two-Piece
Cover:	Surlyn Type
Ball Size:	1.68"
Core:	Solid
Dimples:	432/Icosadodecahedron

Performance Characteristics: The Maxfli Exceptional Spin ball. For the player who wants maximum spin and control without sacrificing distance. A two-piece ball with a scuff-resistant surlyn cover and a high-spin core.

Maxfli XD 90, 100

Manufacturer:	Dunlop Golf Division
Construction:	Two-Piece
Cover:	Surlyn
Ball Size:	1.68"
Core:	Solid
Dimples:	432/Icosadodecahedron

Performance Characteristics: The Maxfli Exceptional Distance ball. For the player who wants outstanding distance, durability, and a straighter flight path without losing all feel. It offers flight stability for longer, straighter shots. A two-piece ball with a durable surlyn cover and high velocity core.

RAM Golf

RAM Golden Girl

Manufacturer:	Hansberger Precision Golf
Construction:	Two-Piece
Cover:	Surlyn
Ball Size:	1.68"
Core:	Solid
Dimples:	442

Performance Characteristics: The Ram Golden Girl is a ball designed for maximum distance, longer carry and better control. A durable multi-colored ball. A Lithium-Surlyn covered ball designed with a high energy core with a dimple pattern for more lift. Available in 80 compression too.

RAM Tour Lite

Manufacturer:	Hansberger Precision Golf
Construction:	Two-Piece
Cover:	Surlyn
Ball Size:	1.68"
Core:	Solid
Dimples:	442

Performance Characteristics: For golfers with slower swing speed (under 80 mph) who want more distance and control. The Lite weight two grams less then a normal golf ball and features a patented double dimple design and soft surlyn cover for more feel.

RAM Tour TDX 150

Manufacturer:	Hansberger Precision Golf
Construction:	Two-Piece
Cover:	Surlyn
Ball Size:	1.68"
Core:	Solid
Dimples:	380/Toroidal

Performance Characteristics: One of Ram's newer balls, a unique toroidal dimple design that enhances the turbulent boundary around the ball and contributes to longer hang time. Most of the total distance achieved is carry. A precise "target" ball. It also has a cut resistant Surlyn cover.

RAM Tour XDC 90, 100

Manufacturer:	Hansberger Precision Golf
Construction:	Two-Piece
Cover:	Lithium Surlyn
Ball Size:	1.68"
Core:	Solid
Dimples:	442/Triangle & Pentagonal

Performance Characteristics: The Ram Tour XDC is a ball designed for the golfer who is looking for distance and durability. XDC's Explosive Distance Core and slight higher launch angle produces longer carry, distance and improved bite on the green. The 442 seamless dimple pattern provides a more accurate and stable flight pattern, even in high wind conditions. Guaranteed cut-proof cover.

RAM Tour Balata LB 90, 100

Manufacturer:	Hansberger Precision Golf
Construction:	Two-Piece
Cover:	Lithium Balata
Ball Size:	1.68"
Core:	Solid
Dimples:	442

Performance Characteristics: The new Pro-Spin 9000 Ram Tour Balata LB is designed for the ultimate in flight control. Testing has proven that 9000 revolutions per minute is the optimum spin rate for shots hit with a pitching wedge. The new Ram Tour Balata LB provides the ideal spin rate and control demanded by tour players and low handicap golfers. It's a ball designed for high spin and medium trajectory. A cut proof cover that is designed to give you feel, spin and control. A seamless dimple design.

RAM Tour Balata DC 90, 100

Manufacturer:	Hansberger Precision Golf
Construction:	Two-Piece Double Cover
Cover:	Lithium Balata
Ball Size:	1.68"
Core:	Solid
Dimples:	442

Performance Characteristics: The new double cover Ram Tour Balata DC provides exceptional performance and durability for the demanding golfer. The highly energized core is the source of the ball's power. The soft inner layer provides unsurpassed feel and control. A firm outer balata cover gives golfers added distance off the tee.

RAM Tour OS 172 90

Manufacturer:	Hansberger Precision Golf
Construction:	Two-Piece
Cover:	Surlyn
Ball Size:	1.72"
Core:	Solid
Dimples:	442
Competition:	Top Flite Magna

Performance Characteristics: An oversized ball similar to the Top-Flite Magna, designed for a lower spin rate for straighter shots. A ball designed for long distance and medium to high trajectory. Most of the distance is achieved in carry with very little run. The ball is extremely durable. The 90 compression is between 90 and 100. The 100 compression is between 100 and 110.

Spalding Sports Worldwide

Molitor 442

Manufacturer: Spalding Sports Worldwide
Construction: Two-Piece
Cover: Surlyn
Ball Size: 1.68"
Core: Solid
Dimples: 442

Performance Characteristics: The Molitor 442 is a ball designed for the average golfer who is looking to achieve distance. It has an improved dimple pattern over the Molitor 332 which provides better flight stability and quicker on the green.

Top-Flite Aero

Manufacturer: Spalding Sports Worldwide
Construction: Two-Piece
Cover: Ionomer (surlyn like)
Ball Size: 1.68"
Core: Solid
Dimples: 332 ellipsoid pattern

Performance Characteristics: Top-Flite's newest ball which is designed for the avid golfer. It features a unique non-circular dimple design with tear drop and ellipsoid shaped dimples to reduce drag and increase distance. Top-Flite claims this is the softest feeling two-piece performance golf ball delivering maximum feel, distance and durability for consistent performance shot-after-shot.

Top-Flite Strata Tour 90, 100

Manufacturer: Spalding Sports Worldwide
Construction: Two-Piece Multi-Layer
Cover: ZS Balata, .050" thick
Second Layer: Mantle Layer .055" thick
Ball Size: 1.68"
Core: Solid, 1.47"
Dimples: 422/Triangle-dimple
Competition: Titleist Tour Balata, Titleist Professional, Maxfli HT

Performance Characteristics: A ball designed for the professional and/or advanced players. It has a multi-layer construction consisting of a soft core, enveloped by a firm inner layer with a balata like cover. It produces lower spin rates off woods and long irons for distance. Produces a higher spin rate off short irons with exceptional feel on greens. The cover is more durable than wound balata golf balls.

Top-Flite Strata Advance 90, 100

Manufacturer:	Spalding Sports Worldwide
Construction:	Two-Piece Multi-Layer
Cover:	Z Balata, .055" thick
Second Layer:	Mantle Layer, HyperElasitc, 075" thick
Ball Size:	1.68"
Core:	Solid, 1.42"
Dimples:	422/Triangle-dimple
Competition:	Titleist DT Wound, Titleist HP2 Tour, Precept EV Extra Spin

Performance Characteristics: A ball designed for the professional and/or advanced players. It has a multi-layer construction consisting of a HyperElastic inner layer between core and soft, shear-resistant balata like cover. It produces distance off both woods and irons. Provides a balata like feel with advanced spin and control around the green. The cover is more durable than wound balata golf balls.

Top-Flite Z-Balata 90, 100

Manufacturer:	Spalding Sports Worldwide
Construction:	Two-Piece
Cover:	Zylin (Surlyn like)
Ball Size:	1.68"
Core:	Solid
Dimples:	332/Icosahedral

Performance Characteristics: Designed for the low handicap players. An extremely soft, yet shear-resistant cover providing exceptional combination of spin, feel and control. Retains spin longer than wound balls. Cut and scuff resistant for better durability.

Top-Flite XL Titanium 90, 100

Manufacturer:	Spalding Sports Worldwide
Construction:	Two-Piece
Cover:	Titanium-based cover material (Surlyn like)
Ball Size:	1.68"
Core:	Solid
Dimples:	422/Triangle-dimple

Performance Characteristics: A titanium-based cover ball designed for players who demand extra long distance form a compression-rated ball. Contains a titanium-enhanced cover material with strengthened chemical bonds. The firm, high energy core provides distance off the tee. Its dimple design gives tour-type trajectory for extra carry and roll.

Top-Flite HOT XL 90, 100

Manufacturer:	Spalding Sports Worldwide
Construction:	Two-Piece
Cover:	Zylin (surlyn like)
Ball Size:	1.68"
Core:	Solid
Dimples:	492/Triangle dimple design

Performance Characteristics: Designed for any player who wants the longest overall distance from a golf ball. Contains an explosive high energy core giving you longer tee-to-green than any other legal golf ball. Extremely durable for extended play.

Top-Flite XL Performance 90, 100

Manufacturer:	Spalding Sports Worldwide
Construction:	Two-Piece
Cover:	Zylin
Ball Size:	1.68"
Core:	Solid
Dimples:	422/Triangle dimple

Performance Characteristics: A ball designed for distance with extra spin and feel. Extra performance in a tour trajectory. A distance ball that provides extra performance benefits for better overall playability. Durable cover for extended play.

Top-Flite XL Tour Trajectory

Manufacturer:	Spalding Sports Worldwide
Construction:	Two-Piece
Cover:	Zylin
Ball Size:	1.68"
Core:	Solid
Dimples:	422/Triangle

Performance Characteristics: This golf ball is designed for golfers who desire pinpoint control and like the way wound balls play. It has a 422 tri-dimple design and a soft resilient Zylin cover the lets the ball hang high over the target and land softly with the spin rate of wound Surlyn golf balls.

Top-Flite XL High Trajectory

Manufacturer:	Spalding Sports Worldwide
Construction:	Two-Piece
Cover:	Zylin
Ball Size:	1.68"
Core:	Solid, Approximately 1.54" Dia
Dimples:	410/Octahelix

Performance Characteristics: A softer feel ball, the spiral 410 octahelix dimple pattern provides a higher trajectory golf ball. It has a durable resilient Zylin cover which allows for more control. It is ideal for 90 compression players. It is available in Spalding's patented Whiter-than-white and High-Visibility orange, yellow, and pink.

Top-Flite XL Regular Trajectory

Manufacturer:	Spalding Sports Worldwide
Construction:	Two-Piece
Cover:	Zylin
Ball Size:	1.68"
Core:	Solid
Dimples:	422/Hexagon

Performance Characteristics: This ball is designed to play in the wind and for increased iron distance. It has a 422 hex dimple design that contains six hexangular arrays mirrored with six triangles to increase the balance of the ball. It has a thinner Zylin cover for better control.

Top-Flite XL-W

Manufacturer:	Spalding Sports Worldwide
Construction:	Two-Piece
Cover:	Zylin
Ball Size:	1.68"
Core:	Solid
Dimples:	410

Performance Characteristics: A ball designed for the swing pattern of a lady. A thin cut-proof Surlyn cover. This is a distance and high trajectory ball with a shallow dimple pattern.

Top-Flite Magna Distance 90,100

Manufacturer:	Spalding Sports Worldwide
Construction:	Two-Piece
Cover:	Zylin
Ball Size:	1.72"
Core:	Solid
Dimples:	422/Tri

Performance Characteristics: A distance ball that is 2% larger in diameter and designed for the serious golfer looking to reduce hooks and slices. Resilient cover material and responsive core designed to provide maximum distance for players with average clubhead speeds. Tour type trajectory for extra carry and roll.

Tad Moore Golf Inc.

Srixon Hi-Spin

Manufacturer:	Tad Moore Golf Inc.
Construction:	Two-Piece
Cover:	Ionomer blend
Ball Size:	1.68"
Core:	Solid
Dimples:	420

General Information: A soft cover delivers excellent spin for shot control. Soft, hi-velocity core provides short-game feel and distance off the tee. Dimple pattern has four sizes; for aerodynamic stability in all wind conditions.

Srixon Hi-Brid

Manufacturer:	Tad Moore Golf Inc.
Construction:	Three-Piece
Cover:	Elastomer-ionomer blend
Ball Size:	1.68"
Core:	Wound Core
Dimples:	410

General Information: High-energy oversized center for distance. Thin latex-thread mid-layer for click and feel better players prefer. Has a solid polystyrene resin center. Is the largest wound ball center; 30% larger than conventional centers for maximum initial velocity. The cover provides excellent spin, yet is durable.

Wilson Sporting Goods

Wilson Staff Titanium Balata 90, 100

Manufacturer:	Wilson Sporting Goods
Construction:	Two-Piece Double Cover
Cover:	Balata Outer Cover
	Magnesium Inner Cover
Ball Size:	1.68"
Core:	Solid
Dimples:	500 ellipsoid dimple pattern

General Information: A titanium core ball too maximize energy transfer at impact. Designed to deliver ultimate feel and control for the low-mid handicap player. It has a double cover. The balata outer cover is designed for feel and control. The magnesium inner cover is designed for greater distance. The dimple pattern is designed to allow the ball to fly longer, lower and bore through the wind.

Wilson Staff Titanium Spin 90, 100

Manufacturer:	Wilson Sporting Goods
Construction:	Two-Piece
Cover:	Magnesium Surlyn Cover
Ball Size:	1.68"
Core:	Solid
Dimples:	500 ellipsoid dimple pattern
Competition:	Titleist HP2 Tour, Titleist DT Wound,

Precept EV Extra Spin, Maxfli XS, Top-Flite Tour SD

General Information: A titanium core ball too maximize energy transfer at impact. Designed to deliver high spin and distance for the low-mid handicap player. The soft magnesium surlyn cover is designed for softer feel and longer distance. The dimple pattern is designed to allow the ball to fly longer, lower and bore through the wind.

Wilson Staff Titanium Distance 90, 100

Manufacturer:	Wilson Sporting Goods
Construction:	Two-Piece
Cover:	Magnesium Surlyn Cover
Ball Size:	1.68"
Core:	Solid
Dimples:	500 ellipsoid dimple pattern
Competition:	Titleist HP2 Distance, Titleist DT 2-Piece, Precept EV Extra, Distance, Maxfli XD

General Information: A titanium core ball too maximize energy transfer at impact. Designed to deliver maximum distance for the mid-high handicap player. The magnesium surlyn cover is designed for softer feel and longer distance. The dimple pattern is designed to allow the ball to fly longer, lower and bore through the wind.

Ultra 500 Competition 90, 100

Manufacturer:	Wilson Sporting Goods
Construction:	Two-Piece
Cover:	Lithium Surlyn and Zinc
Ball Size:	1.68"
Core:	Solid
Dimples:	500/Geodesic Icosahedral

Performance Characteristics: A ball designed for high spin and distance. It's dimple pattern contains three types of dimple sizes, shapes and depths for optimal aerodynamics. It delivers maximum distance with a high spin rate for the low-mid handicap player who desires a ball with more maneuverability without sacrificing distance or durability. It has a no-cut guarantee cover.

Ultra 500 Tour Balata 90, 100

Manufacturer:	Wilson Sporting Goods
Construction:	Two-Piece
Cover:	Balata
Ball Size:	1.68"
Core:	Solid
Dimples:	500/Geodesic Icosahedral

Performance Characteristics: A ball designed for ultimate feel and distance. It's dimple pattern contains three types of dimple sizes, shapes and depths for optimal aerodynamics. It delivers ultimate feel and distance for the low-mid handicap player who desires control and maneuverability with unsurpassed balata durability.

Ultra 500 Distance 90, 100

Manufacturer:	Wilson Sporting Goods
Construction:	Two-Piece
Cover:	Surlyn
Ball Size:	1.68"
Core:	Solid
Dimples:	500/Geodesic Icosahedral

Performance Characteristics: A ball designed for maximum distance. It's dimple pattern contains three types of dimple sizes, shapes and depths for optimal aerodynamics. It delivers maximum distance with a low spin rate for the mid-high handicap player whose play objective is longer distance. It has a no-cut guarantee cover.

Ultra 500 Double Cover

Manufacturer:	Wilson Sporting Goods
Construction:	Two-Piece, Double Cover
Cover:	Soft Surlyn
Ball Size:	1.68"
Core:	Solid
Dimples:	500/Geodesic Icosahedral

Performance Characteristics: A ball designed for feel, control and distance. Excellent feel. A two-piece double cover ball with a soft surlyn cover.

Ultra 500 Women's

Manufacturer:	Wilson Sporting Goods
Construction:	Two-Piece
Cover:	Soft Surlyn
Ball Size:	1.68"
Core:	Solid
Dimples:	500/Geodesic Icosahedral

Performance Characteristics: A ball designed for maximum distance and high trajectory. This two-piece ball has a durable cover for distance and accuracy.

Ultra DPS Original 90, 100

Manufacturer:	Wilson Sporting Goods
Construction:	Two-Piece
Cover:	Surlyn
Ball Size:	1.68"
Core:	Solid
Dimples:	432/Icosahedral

Performance Characteristics: The Ultra Distance Performance Series (DPS) is designed for distance with specific performance features for each player type. The Original has a high energy core for maximum distance. It has a cut proof surlyn cover for ultimate durability. Delivers a combination of maximum distance and durability for the mid-high handicap player. It has a no-cut guarantee cover.

Ultra DPS Tour Spin 90, 100

Manufacturer:	Wilson Sporting Goods
Construction:	Two-Piece
Cover:	Surlyn
Ball Size:	1.68"
Core:	Solid
Dimples:	432/Icosahedral

Performance Characteristics: The Ultra Distance Performance Series (DPS) is designed for distance with specific performance features for each player type. The Tour Spin features a larger high energy core for distance, with a thin soft surlyn cover for extra spin and feel. Delivers a combination of maximum distance and spin for the mid-high handicap player who desires a ball with more control without sacrificing distance. It has a no-cut guarantee cover.

Ultra DPS Classic Wound 90, 100

Manufacturer: Wilson Sporting Goods
Construction: Three-Piece
Cover: Surlyn
Ball Size: 1.68"
Core: Wound solid center
Dimples: 432/Icosahedral

Performance Characteristics: The Ultra Distance Performance Series (DPS) is designed for distance with specific performance features for each player type. The Classic Wound features a small solid center and dense windings to produce a 3-piece ball with superior control and maximum bite. Delivers a combination of feel and control with maximum durability for the low-mid handicap player. It has a no-cut guarantee cover.

Wilson TC2 Distance

Manufacturer: Wilson Sporting Goods
Construction: Two-Piece
Cover: Surlyn
Ball Size: 1.68"
Core: Solid
Dimples: 432 Truncated Cone Dimple Design

Performance Characteristics: A 2-piece cut proof Surlyn ball for durability designed for the mid-high handicap golfer. The high energy core is designed for initial maximum velocity, distance off the tee. A truncated cone dimple design utilizing five dimple sizes, symmetrically positioned to give in-flight stability.

Wilson TC2 Tour

Manufacturer: Wilson Sporting Goods
Construction: Two-Piece
Cover: Surlyn
Ball Size: 1.68"
Core: Solid
Dimples: 432 Truncated Cone Dimple Design

Performance Characteristics: A 2-piece cut proof Surlyn ball for durability designed for the mid-high handicap golfer. The high energy core is designed for initial maximum velocity, distance off the tee and control onto the green. A truncated cone dimple design utilizing five dimple sizes, symmetrically positioned to give in-flight stability.

ProStaff Distance

Manufacturer:	Wilson Sporting Goods
Construction:	Two-Piece
Cover:	Surlyn
Ball Size:	1.68"
Core:	Solid
Dimples:	432

Performance Characteristics: A ball designed for maximum distance and durability. For serious golfers who desire maximum distance and accuracy. The cover is high resilience surlyn for durability. A high energy core for distance.

ProStaff Control

Manufacturer:	Wilson Sporting Goods
Construction:	Three-Piece
Cover:	Surlyn
Ball Size:	1.68"
Core:	Wound Solid Center
Dimples:	432

Performance Characteristics: A ball designed for maximum distance with enhanced maneuverability. For traditional golfers who desire a 3-piece ball for softer feel and more maneuverability without compromising distance. A high resilience surlyn cover for durability. The core is wound center for control and feel. It has a truncated cone dimple design.

ProStaff Tour Trajectory

Manufacturer:	Wilson Sporting Goods
Construction:	Two-Piece
Cover:	Surlyn
Ball Size:	1.68"
Core:	Solid
Dimples:	432

Performance Characteristics: A ball designed for maximum distance and low flight pattern. For golfers who desire a low launch angle and more control. Excellent for windy conditions. A high resilience surlyn cover for durability. A high energy core for distance. It has a truncated cone dimple design.

ProStaff Performance/Spin

Manufacturer:	Wilson Sporting Goods
Construction:	Two-Piece
Cover:	Surlyn
Ball Size:	1.68"
Core:	Solid
Dimples:	432

Performance Characteristics: A ball designed to give enhanced spin for more control and a soft cover for more feel. For golfers who desire extra spin for better ball control around the greens and with iron shots. A soft surlyn cover for feel and control. A high energy core for distance.

ProStaff Distance-W

Manufacturer:	Wilson Sporting Goods
Construction:	Two-Piece
Cover:	Surlyn
Ball Size:	1.68"
Core:	Solid
Dimples:	432

Performance Characteristics: A ball that is designed for a lady's swing pattern and strength. Provides maximum distance and is designed for a slower swing speed. For women golfers who desire maximum distance and accuracy. A high resilience surlyn cover for durability. A women's compression core for better feel.

ProStaff Distance-Sr

Manufacturer:	Wilson Sporting Goods
Construction:	Two-Piece
Cover:	Surlyn
Ball Size:	1.68"
Core:	Solid
Dimples:	432

Performance Characteristics: A ball designed for a senior's swing pattern and strength. Provides maximum distance and is designed for a slower swing speed. For senior golfers who desire maximum distance and accuracy. A high resilience surlyn cover for durability. A senior's compression core for better feel.

Golf Balls - Independent Test Results

There are many more brands and types of golf balls on the shelves these days because this is what manufacturers are saying most golfers want -- a golf ball for individual styles and levels of play.

Just what are they telling us we should be looking for when buying the right golf ball to fit our style of play?

Now you need to know such things as your club head speed, whether or not you are a low, medium or high handicap golfer, and whether you want a ball built strictly for distance or one that you can feel and control. This certainly is a different marketing strategy from the days not all that long ago when the makers were selling us on strictly distance.

To help you understand the many differences between the golf balls of today, we conducted an independent performance test using the latest and most popular golf balls available on the market today. Outlined below is our testing methodology followed by the results of the test.

Testing Criteria

The golf balls used in our test were purchased from various on-course and off-course golf shops. This included a small sampling of 90 and 100 compression balls of the same type. Prior to testing, each golf ball was placed into one of the four performance groups:

- **Distance/Durability Golf Balls** - for players who place the highest value on distance and durability of the ball and its cover.

- Feel/Distance/Durability Golf Balls - for players who are interested in a blend of distance and durability with a softer touch and feel to the ball.

- Spin/Feel/Durability Golf Balls - for the high performance player who seeks feel and higher spin rates for control when hitting the ball.

- Spin/Feel/Balata Golf Balls - for the high performance player who seeks feel and higher spin rates for control when hitting the ball with the exception that the cover is balata or balata mix with less durability.

An independent testing facility designed specifically for testing all outdoor golf equipment was used. Our golf balls were tested under a controlled and wind free environment using proven testing methods to ensure consistency and quality results. Using a custom built electro-mechanical hitting machine (a robot) equipped with a golf club of choice, performance data was collected for every ball hit. Club head and ball velocity were measured using Oehler speed gauges.

For every ball type tested, the same sample size was used. Each ball of the same type was hit identically off the machine and their data recorded. The data collected was then used to determine the ball's performance, accuracy and construction consistency.

Golf Balls Tested

DISTANCE/DURABILITY GOLF BALLS

DUNLOP DDH 110	PRECEPT EV LADY	TOPFLITE MAGNA DISTANCE 90
DUNLOP DDH FOR WOMEN	PROSTAFF DISTANCE	TOPFLITE XL 90 TITANIUM
G. NORMAN SHARK DIST.	RAM TOUR XDC 90	ULTRA 500 DISTANCE 90
MAXFLI XD 100	SLAZ 420D RAW DIST. PLUS	ULTRA DPS ORIGINAL
MAXFLI XD 90	TITLEIST DT 2 PIECE	WILSON STAFF TI DIST 90
PINNACLE EQUALIZER	TITLEIST HP-2 DISTANCE	WILSON TC2 TOUR
PRECEPT EV EXTRA DIST	TOPFLITE HOT XL REG TRJ	

FEEL/DISTANCE/DURABILITY GOLF BALLS

DUNLOP DDH CONTROL PLUS	SRIXON HI-BRID 3 PIECE	TOPFLITE STRATA ADVANCED 90
PRECEPT DYNAWING	TITLEIST HP-2 TOUR	ULTRA 500 COMPETITION 90
PRECEPT EV SENIOR	TITLEIST TOUR DISTANCE 90	
SLAZ 420P POWER CONTROL	TOPFLITE AERO	

SPIN/FEEL/DURABILITY GOLF BALLS

DUNLOP DDH SPIN PLUS	PROSTAFF PERFORM. SPIN	TOPFLITE STRATA TOUR 90
G. NORMAN SHARK SPIN	SLAZ 420T TOUR CALIBRE	TOPFLITE XL PERFORMANCE 90
MAXFLI XS100	SRIXON HI-SPIN 2 PIECE	ULTRA DPS TOUR SPIN
PRECEPT EV EXTRA SPIN	TITLEIST DT WOUND 90	WILSON STAFF TITANIUM SPIN 90
PRECEPT TOUR DBLE COVER	TITLEIST PROFESSIONAL 90	

SPIN/FEEL/BALATA GOLF BALLS

MAXFLI HT BALATA 100	RAM TOUR BALATA DC 100	TITLEIST TOUR BALATA
MAXFLI HT BALATA 90	RAM TOUR BALATA DC 90	WILSON STAFF TI BALATA 90
MAXFLI XF100 BALATA	RAM TOUR BALATA LB 100	

Testing Parameters

Following are the definitions of the testing parameters used for the test. Once all balls selected for the independent test were placed in their appropriated Performance Group, the same tests were performed for each ball at 80, 90 and 100 mph swing speeds.

Performance Group
All balls tested were grouped into one of the four performance groups:

- Distance/Durability Golf Balls
- Feel/Distance/Durability Golf Balls
- Spin/Feel/Durability Golf Balls
- Spin/Feel/Balata Golf Balls

Club/Shaft
To represent what most of the average golfers are using today, we conducted the test using an oversized driver. For each test, the Taylor Made Burner 10.5° driver with a 10.5° loft, 58.0° lie, 0.0° face angle, D3 swing weight, and a regular steel shaft was used.

Ball Type
The construction type of the ball. 2P represents a two-piece ball, 2PDC represents a two-piece double-cover ball, 3P represents a three-piece ball, and 3PDC represents a three-piece double-cover ball.

Launch Angle
Measured in degrees, this is the initial launch angle of the ball off the club head at that speed.

Total Carry

Measured in yards, the total distance of the ball while in flight.

Total Distance

Measured in yards, the total distance of the ball's carry and roll.

Carry and Total Dispersion

This ranking represents the accuracy of how straight the ball stayed on target for total carry and total distance. This is a measurement that is either left or right from a centerline that is perpendicular from where the ball is launched. This measurement is relative to the manufacturing quality and consistency of the golf ball and its ability to hold a straight line toward the target. A golf ball measuring in feet between:

- 0' to 5' from the centerline is rated: A
- 6' to 10' from the centerline is rated: B
- 11' to 15' from the centerline is rated: C
- 16' or more from the centerline is rated: D

Ball Velocity

At the point of impact of the ball leaving the club head, the speed of the ball in feet per second.

Trajectory

The curved path of the ball while in flight. Trajectory is measured through a wire screen with one inch square increments. The range is from zero to ten. The number is recorded at the point which the ball reaches its apex. These numbers are for reference only to other balls in the same test.

80 MPH Swing Speed - Ranked by Distance

CLUB / SHAFT: OVERSIZED DRIVER, 10.5 DEGREE LOFT, REGULAR STEEL SHAFT

PERFORMANCE GROUP: DISTANCE/DURABILITY BALLS

	Ball Type	Total Dist	Carry Dist	Carry Disp.	Total Disp.	Launch Angle	Ball Velocity	Traj.
PRECEPT EV LADY	2P	196.50	176.50	B	B	12.34	174.05	6.88
ULTRA 500 DISTANCE 90	2P	195.50	177.67	B	B	12.44	175.77	6.77
TOPFLITE MAGNA DISTANCE 90	2P	195.17	175.67	B	B	12.54	174.13	6.85
SLAZ 420D RAW DISTANCE PLUS	2P	195.00	177.33	B	B	12.17	174.90	6.87
TOPFLITE XL 90 TITANIUM	2P	195.00	176.67	A	A	12.17	174.28	6.78
TITLEIST DT 2 PIECE	2P	194.83	176.00	B	B	12.50	173.95	6.53
TOPFLITE HOT XL REG TRAJ	2P	194.67	175.33	B	C	12.17	173.67	6.62
PINNACLE EQUALIZER	2P	194.33	176.00	A	B	12.10	175.12	6.83
PRECEPT EV EXTRA DISTANCE	2P	193.67	176.83	B	B	12.44	174.33	6.97
PROSTAFF DISTANCE	2P	193.67	176.67	A	C	12.00	174.90	6.73
UTLRA DPS ORIGINAL	2P	193.33	177.50	B	C	12.00	175.62	6.88
DUNLOP DDH FOR WOMEN	2P	192.50	177.00	B	C	12.27	175.78	7.25
MAXFLI XD 90	2P	192.33	175.67	A	B	12.00	175.13	6.72
DUNLOP DDH 110	2P	191.83	175.67	B	B	12.17	174.20	7.03
WILSON STAFF TI DISTANCE 90	2P	191.67	177.33	A	A	11.96	175.25	6.88
MAXFLI XD 100	2P	190.83	176.83	B	B	12.00	175.08	6.73
TITLEIST HP-2 DISTANCE	2P	189.50	173.83	A	A	12.37	173.05	6.83
WILSON TC2 TOUR	2P	189.33	178.00	A	B	11.82	175.10	7.00
GREG NORMAN SHARK DISTANCE	2P	188.67	175.67	A	A	11.90	174.92	6.90
RAM TOUR XDC 90	2P	186.50	170.33	B	B	11.20	171.75	6.82

PERFORMANCE GROUP: FEEL/DIST/DURABILITY BALLS

	Ball Type	Total Dist	Carry Dist	Carry Disp.	Total Disp.	Launch Angle	Ball Velocity	Traj.
SLAZ 420P POWER CONTROL	2P	196.67	176.67	A	B	12.37	174.78	6.85
TITLEIST TOUR DISTANCE 90	3P	195.50	169.50	A	B	12.30	170.93	6.30
TITLEIST HP-2 TOUR	2P	195.17	169.67	A	B	12.03	170.98	6.47
TOPFLITE AERO	2P	194.67	174.33	B	B	12.17	173.15	6.85
PRECEPT EV SENIOR	2P	193.33	176.50	A	B	12.17	174.37	6.88
SRIXON HI-BRID 3 PIECE	3P	192.17	174.17	B	C	11.60	173.35	6.65
PRECEPT DYNAWING	2PDC	190.33	174.50	B	B	12.65	173.05	6.95
ULTRA 500 COMPETITION 90	2P	190.17	172.33	A	A	12.00	173.18	6.70
TOPFLITE STRATA ADVANCED 90	2PDC	188.67	172.83	B	B	12.00	172.67	6.63
DUNLOP DDH CONTROL PLUS	2P	185.67	174.83	B	B	12.65	175.52	7.50

PERFORMANCE GROUP: SPIN/FEEL/DURABILITY BALLS

	Ball Type	Total Dist	Carry Dist	Carry Disp.	Total Disp.	Launch Angle	Ball Velocity	Traj.
PROSTAFF PERFORMANCE SPIN	2P	197.17	174.33	A	B	12.17	173.50	6.65
DUNLOP DDH SPIN PLUS	2P	195.17	174.00	B	B	12.44	173.32	6.67
SLAZ 420T TOUR CALIBRE	2P	194.50	174.67	B	B	12.17	173.58	6.75
WILSON STAFF TI SPIN 90	2P	194.33	172.83	A	A	12.34	172.38	6.58

80 mph continrued - **PERFORMANCE GROUP: SPIN/FEEL/DURABILITY BALLS**

	Ball Type	Total Dist	Carry Dist	Carry Disp.	Total Disp.	Launch Angle	Ball Velocity	Traj.
TOPFLITE XL PERFORMANCE 90	2P	193.67	174.33	A	A	12.37	172.80	6.77
PRECEPT EV EXTRA SPIN	2P	193.33	173.67	B	A	12.23	172.57	6.88
ULTRA DPS TOUR SPIN	2P	193.17	174.83	B	B	12.50	173.08	6.70
MAXFLI XS 100	2P	192.83	172.17	A	B	12.37	171.80	6.47
PRECEPT TOUR DOUBLE COVER	3PDC	192.33	172.50	A	B	12.17	172.28	6.63
TITLEIST PROFESSIONAL 90	3P	192.00	168.50	A	B	12.17	171.20	6.35
GREG NORMAN SHARK SPIN	2P	190.83	174.17	B	C	11.96	172.97	6.62
TOPFLITE STRATA TOUR 90	2PDC	190.17	171.33	B	B	12.00	171.50	6.45
TITLEIST DT WOUND 90	3P	189.50	170.83	A	B	11.69	171.50	6.62
SRIXON HI-SPIN 2 PIECE	2P	185.33	170.17	B	B	12.10	172.40	7.13

PERFORMANCE GROUP: SPIN/FEEL/BALATA BALLS

	Ball Type	Total Dist	Carry Dist	Carry Disp.	Total Disp.	Launch Angle	Ball Velocity	Traj.
WILSON STAFF TI BALATA 90	2PDC	190.83	171.83	B	B	12.50	172.55	6.40
RAM TOUR BALATA DC 90	2PDC	190.50	171.00	A	B	11.75	171.05	6.63
TITLEIST TOUR BALATA	3P	190.40	164.20	A	A	12.17	163.24	6.54
RAM TOUR BALATA DC 100	2PDC	188.83	171.50	B	B	12.34	172.92	6.88
MAXFLI HT BALATA 100	3P	187.00	165.50	A	B	12.34	169.00	5.97
RAM TOUR BALATA LB 100	2P	186.50	169.83	A	B	12.44	170.83	6.52
MAXFLI XF 100 DURABLE BALATA	3P	185.50	165.50	A	B	11.55	169.97	6.22
MAXFLI HT BALATA 90	3P	185.00	162.50	A	C	11.80	167.38	5.85

90 MPH Swing Speed - Ranked by Distance

CLUB / SHAFT: OVERSIZED DRIVER, 10.5 DEGREE LOFT, REGULAR STEEL SHAFT

PERFORMANCE GROUP: DISTANCE/DURABILITY BALLS

	Ball Type	Total Dist	Carry Dist	Carry Disp.	Total Disp.	Launch Angle	Ball Velocity	Traj.
TOPFLITE XL 90 TITANIUM	2P	229.83	205.17	B	C	10.90	195.27	6.58
ULTRA 500 DISTANCE 90	2P	227.50	204.33	A	C	11.00	197.30	6.37
MAXFLI XD 100	2P	227.00	202.83	A	B	10.50	196.10	6.43
PRECEPT EV LADY	2P	226.50	205.33	B	C	10.50	195.13	6.47
MAXFLI XD 90	2P	225.33	201.83	B	B	10.60	196.22	6.58
PINNACLE EQUALIZER	2P	225.00	202.67	B	C	10.50	196.10	6.53
TOPFLITE MAGNA DISTANCE 90	2P	224.50	202.50	A	A	10.24	195.17	6.58
PROSTAFF DISTANCE	2P	224.33	205.00	B	C	10.30	195.93	6.53
TOPFLITE HOT XL REG TRAJ	2P	224.17	202.83	B	B	10.30	194.90	6.37
GREG NORMAN SHARK DISTANCE	2P	223.83	205.83	B	C	10.55	196.48	6.75
TITLEIST DT 2 PIECE	2P	223.83	202.83	B	B	11.00	195.07	6.52
SLAZ 420D RAW DISTANCE PLUS	2P	223.33	204.83	A	B	10.60	195.97	6.82

90 mph continued - **PERFORMANCE GROUP: DISTANCE/DURABILITY BALLS**

	Ball Type	Total Dist	Carry Dist	Carry Disp.	Total Disp.	Launch Angle	Ball Velocity	Traj.
UTLRA DPS ORIGINAL	2P	222.33	204.00	B	C	10.40	196.47	6.58
TITLEIST HP-2 DISTANCE	2P	222.33	203.00	A	C	10.34	194.35	6.78
DUNLOP DDH 110	2P	221.50	205.50	A	B	10.44	196.02	6.87
DUNLOP DDH FOR WOMEN	2P	221.00	206.50	B	C	10.30	197.82	7.15
WILSON TC2 TOUR	2P	221.00	206.50	B	C	11.14	196.38	6.73
PRECEPT EV EXTRA DISTANCE	2P	220.33	205.50	A	B	10.80	195.28	6.82
WILSON STAFF TI DISTANCE 90	2P	218.83	203.50	A	B	10.20	197.03	6.33
RAM TOUR XDC 90	2P	216.00	200.33	B	B	10.50	192.08	6.58

PERFORMANCE GROUP: FEEL/DIST/DURABILITY BALLS

	Ball Type	Total Dist	Carry Dist	Carry Disp.	Total Disp.	Launch Angle	Ball Velocity	Traj.
TOPFLITE AERO	2P	226.33	201.00	B	B	10.60	193.47	6.55
PRECEPT EV SENIOR	2P	224.83	203.67	B	B	10.40	195.00	6.50
SLAZ 420P POWER CONTROL	2P	223.67	205.50	B	B	10.40	195.88	6.65
DUNLOP DDH CONTROL PLUS	2P	221.50	205.00	B	B	10.60	198.22	7.15
PRECEPT DYNAWING	2PDC	220.67	202.33	B	C	10.55	193.70	6.55
SIXRON HI-BRID 3 PIECE	3P	220.67	200.83	B	C	10.80	193.23	6.40
TITLEIST TOUR DISTANCE 90	3P	220.00	198.83	A	B	10.72	192.15	6.28
TOPFLITE STRATA ADVANCED 90	2PDC	217.83	201.67	B	C	10.00	193.63	6.37
ULTRA 500 COMPETITION 90	2P	216.33	200.00	B	C	10.30	193.95	6.33
TITLEIST HP-2 TOUR	2P	215.50	194.50	B	B	10.27	191.83	6.17

PERFORMANCE GROUP: SPIN/FEEL/DURABILITY BALLS

	Ball Type	Total Dist	Carry Dist	Carry Disp.	Total Disp.	Launch Angle	Ball Velocity	Traj.
MAXFLI XS 100	2P	224.83	198.00	C	C	10.30	192.57	6.28
SLAZ 420T TOUR CALIBRE	2P	223.67	202.83	B	C	10.50	194.10	6.50
TOPFLITE XL PERFORMANCE 90	2P	222.83	201.67	B	C	10.45	193.85	6.37
DUNLOP DDH SPIN PLUS	2P	222.00	202.00	B	B	10.40	194.50	6.52
WILSON STAFF TI SPIN 90	2P	222.00	200.00	B	B	10.34	192.88	6.32
TOPFLITE STRATA TOUR 90	2PDC	221.67	198.50	A	B	10.24	192.15	6.22
PRECEPT TOUR DOUBLE COVER	3PDC	221.67	201.67	A	B	10.00	192.90	6.48
PROSTAFF PERFORMANCE SPIN	2P	221.67	200.33	A	B	10.80	194.07	6.32
TITLEIST PROFESSIONAL 90	3P	221.67	195.17	A	B	10.30	192.93	6.13
TITLEIST DT WOUND 90	3P	221.33	199.83	A	B	10.80	193.63	6.45
GREG NORMAN SHARK SPIN	2P	221.17	201.83	B	C	10.50	194.35	6.33
PRECEPT EV EXTRA SPIN	2P	220.33	202.17	B	C	10.40	192.70	6.62
ULTRA DPS TOUR SPIN	2P	219.33	201.33	B	C	10.30	194.05	6.27
SRIXON HI-SPIN 2 PIECE	2P	218.67	200.67	A	B	10.30	192.77	6.75

PERFORMANCE GROUP: SPIN/FEEL/BALATA BALLS

	Ball Type	Total Dist	Carry Dist	Carry Disp.	Total Disp.	Launch Angle	Ball Velocity	Traj.
MAXFLI HT BALATA 100	3P	219.83	192.50	A	A	10.50	190.77	5.93
RAM TOUR BALATA LB 100	2P	219.50	197.83	B	C	10.30	190.88	6.32

90 mph continued - **PERFORMANCE GROUP: SPIN/FEEL/BALATA BALLS**

	Ball Type	Total Dist	Carry Dist	Carry Disp.	Total Disp.	Launch Angle	Ball Velocity	Traj.
RAM TOUR BALATA DC 100	2PDC	219.17	201.67	B	B	10.10	193.45	6.73
RAM TOUR BALATA DC 90	2PDC	218.50	197.17	C	B	10.80	191.00	6.25
TITLEIST TOUR BALATA 90	3P	217.40	193.60	A	B	10.30	187.54	6.50
MAXFLI HT BALATA 90	3P	216.50	189.00	B	B	10.50	188.43	5.88
MAXFLI XF 100 DURABLE BALATA	3P	216.17	192.00	A	C	10.30	190.25	5.85
WILSON STAFF TI BALATA 90	2PDC	215.50	197.00	B	C	10.60	193.15	6.08

100 MPH Swing Speed - Ranked by Distance
CLUB / SHAFT: OVERSIZED DRIVER, 10.5 DEGREE LOFT, REGULAR STEEL SHAFT

PERFORMANCE GROUP: DISTANCE/DURABILITY BALLS

	Ball Type	Total Dist	Carry Dist	Carry Disp.	Total Disp.	Launch Angle	Ball Velocity	Traj.
TOPFLITE HOT XL REG TRAJ	2P	248.83	230.17	A	B	10.20	211.73	5.42
PRECEPT EV EXTRA DISTANCE	2P	246.00	230.33	B	B	9.60	212.38	6.08
SLAZ 420D RAW DISTANCE PLUS	2P	245.83	230.50	B	B	9.20	212.75	5.83
WILSON TC2 TOUR	2P	245.83	230.33	B	C	8.85	213.47	6.25
WILSON STAFF TI DISTANCE 90	2P	245.50	230.50	B	B	9.50	214.22	5.93
TOPFLITE XL 90 TITANIUM	2P	245.33	230.83	B	C	9.60	212.25	5.68
ULTRA 500 DISTANCE 90	2P	245.00	229.83	A	B	9.40	214.53	5.77
MAXFLI XD 90	2P	244.17	229.83	B	C	9.10	213.38	5.77
PRECEPT EV LADY	2P	243.83	229.67	B	B	9.60	211.98	5.82
MAXFLI XD 100	2P	242.83	229.17	A	B	9.60	213.22	5.70
TITLEIST DT 2 PIECE	2P	242.83	228.83	A	A	9.60	212.28	5.45
PINNACLE EQUALIZER	2P	242.67	227.17	A	C	9.40	213.02	5.85
PROSTAFF DISTANCE	2P	242.33	229.17	A	B	9.30	213.55	5.85
TOPFLITE MAGNA DISTANCE 90	2P	241.67	227.33	A	B	9.50	212.12	5.70
UTLRA DPS ORIGINAL	2P	240.33	228.83	C	C	9.40	213.73	6.03
TITLEIST HP-2 DISTANCE	2P	240.00	229.17	B	C	9.90	211.35	5.77
GREG NORMAN SHARK DISTANCE	2P	240.00	227.83	A	A	9.20	213.18	6.30
DUNLOP DDH 110	2P	236.83	227.83	C	C	9.40	212.37	6.62
RAM TOUR XDC 90	2P	232.33	221.33	C	C	9.40	208.63	6.00
DUNLOP DDH FOR WOMEN	2P	231.83	225.50	C	C	9.75	214.65	7.20

PERFORMANCE GROUP: FEEL/DIST/DURABILITY BALLS

	Ball Type	Total Dist	Carry Dist	Carry Disp.	Total Disp.	Launch Angle	Ball Velocity	Traj.
SLAZ 420P POWER CONTROL	2P	246.50	230.33	D	D	9.60	212.72	5.75
TITLEIST TOUR DISTANCE 90	3P	244.17	225.17	A	B	9.10	209.63	5.30
PRECEPT EV SENIOR	2P	244.00	228.50	B	B	9.90	212.25	5.75
TOPFLITE AERO	2P	242.83	226.67	B	B	9.75	209.95	5.67

100 mph continued - **PERFORMANCE GROUP: FEEL/DIST/DURABILITY BALLS**

	Ball Type	Total Dist	Carry Dist	Carry Disp.	Total Disp.	Launch Angle	Ball Velocity	Traj.
TOPFLITE STRATA ADVANCED 90	2PDC	240.33	226.50	A	A	9.10	210.93	5.80
DUNLOP DDH CONTROL PLUS	2P	239.00	227.00	B	B	9.60	214.85	7.03
TITLEIST HP-2 TOUR	2P	238.50	220.83	A	B	9.30	208.27	5.38
SRIXON HI-BRID 3 PIECE	3P	236.67	225.00	A	B	9.20	210.15	5.73
ULTRA 500 COMPETITION 90	2P	236.67	224.00	B	B	9.20	210.83	5.70
PRECEPT DYNAWING	2PDC	235.67	226.50	C	C	9.40	210.40	6.00

PERFORMANCE GROUP: SPIN/FEEL/DURABILITY BALLS

	Ball Type	Total Dist	Carry Dist	Carry Disp.	Total Disp.	Launch Angle	Ball Velocity	Traj.
ULTRA DPS TOUR SPIN	2P	243.67	226.83	B	B	9.40	211.18	5.77
WILSON STAFF TI SPIN 90	2P	243.33	225.33	B	B	9.30	209.62	5.38
TITLEIST DT WOUND 90	3P	240.33	225.33	A	B	10.80	209.85	5.65
TITLEIST PROFESSIONAL 90	3P	238.33	223.33	B	A	9.30	210.07	5.38
SLAZ 420T TOUR CALIBRE	2P	238.17	226.50	C	C	9.40	210.93	5.88
PRECEPT EV EXTRA SPIN	2P	238.17	223.00	B	B	9.10	209.65	6.18
PRECEPT TOUR DOUBLE COVER	3PDC	237.83	223.33	B	C	9.20	209.67	5.98
TOPFLITE XL PERFORMANCE 90	2P	237.50	225.50	B	B	9.20	210.65	5.85
TOPFLITE STRATA TOUR 90	2PDC	237.33	222.50	B	C	9.10	208.67	5.33
GREG NORMAN SHARK SPIN	2P	237.00	225.50	C	C	9.40	210.77	5.82
MAXFLI XS 100	2P	237.00	222.67	B	B	9.10	209.02	5.57
PROSTAFF PERFORMANCE SPIN	2P	236.83	224.33	B	B	9.60	211.02	5.83
DUNLOP DDH SPIN PLUS	2P	235.00	225.83	C	D	9.20	211.20	6.02
SRIXON HI-SPIN 2 PIECE	2P	230.33	223.83	C	B	9.20	209.78	6.17

PERFORMANCE GROUP: SPIN/FEEL/BALATA BALLS

	Ball Type	Total Dist	Carry Dist	Carry Disp.	Total Disp.	Launch Angle	Ball Velocity	Traj.
TITLEIST TOUR BALATA 90	3P	245.80	220.60	B	B	9.30	206.58	7.00
WILSON STAFF TI BALATA 90	2PDC	239.33	222.83	C	C	9.20	209.77	5.40
RAM TOUR BALATA DC 100	2PDC	237.00	226.00	C	D	9.60	209.95	5.77
MAXFLI HT BALATA 90	3P	234.50	216.83	B	B	9.10	205.23	5.03
RAM TOUR BALATA LB 100	2P	234.33	219.50	B	B	9.10	207.35	5.83
MAXFLI HT BALATA 100	3P	233.17	219.83	B	B	9.20	207.55	5.32
RAM TOUR BALATA DC 90	2PDC	232.50	219.00	C	C	9.30	207.17	5.70
MAXFLI XF 100 DURABLE BALATA	3P	231.83	217.83	B	C	9.10	207.20	5.37

86

80 MPH Swing Speed - Ranked by Distance

CLUB / SHAFT: OVERSIZED DRIVER, 10.5 DEGREE LOFT, REGULAR STEEL SHAFT

ALL BALLS TESTED WITHOUT PERFORMANCE GROUP RATING

	Ball Type	Total Dist	Carry Dist	Carry Disp.	Total Disp.	Launch Angle	Ball Velocity	Traj.
PROSTAFF PERFORMANCE SPIN	2P	197.17	174.33	A	B	12.17	173.50	6.65
SLAZ 420P POWER CONTROL	2P	196.67	176.67	A	B	12.37	174.78	6.85
PRECEPT EV LADY	2P	196.50	176.50	B	B	12.34	174.05	6.88
ULTRA 500 DISTANCE 90	2P	195.50	177.67	B	B	12.44	175.77	6.77
TITLEIST TOUR DISTANCE 90	3P	195.50	169.50	A	B	12.30	170.93	6.30
TOPFLITE MAGNA DISTANCE 90	2P	195.17	175.67	B	B	12.54	174.13	6.85
DUNLOP DDH SPIN PLUS	2P	195.17	174.00	B	B	12.44	173.32	6.67
TITLEIST HP-2 TOUR	2P	195.17	169.67	A	B	12.03	170.98	6.47
SLAZ 420D RAW DISTANCE PLUS	2P	195.00	177.33	B	B	12.17	174.90	6.87
TOPFLITE XL 90 TITANIUM	2P	195.00	176.67	A	A	12.17	174.28	6.78
TITLEIST DT 2 PIECE	2P	194.83	176.00	B	B	12.50	173.95	6.53
TOPFLITE HOT XL REG TRAJ	2P	194.67	175.33	B	C	12.17	173.67	6.62
TOPFLITE AERO	2P	194.67	174.33	B	B	12.17	173.15	6.85
SLAZ 420T TOUR CALIBRE	2P	194.50	174.67	B	B	12.17	173.58	6.75
PINNACLE EQUALIZER	2P	194.33	176.00	A	B	12.10	175.12	6.83
WILSON STAFF TI SPIN 90	2P	194.33	172.83	A	A	12.34	172.38	6.58
PRECEPT EVE EXTRA DISTANCE	2P	193.67	176.83	B	B	12.44	174.33	6.97
PROSTAFF DISTANCE	2P	193.67	176.67	A	C	12.00	174.90	6.73
TOPFLITE XL 90 PERFORMANCE	2P	193.67	174.33	A	A	12.37	172.80	6.77
UTLRA DPS ORIGINAL	2P	193.33	177.50	B	C	12.00	175.62	6.88
PRECEPT EV SENIOR	2P	193.33	176.50	A	B	12.17	174.37	6.88
PRECEPT EV EXTRA SPIN	2P	193.33	173.67	B	A	12.23	172.57	6.88
ULTRA DPS TOUR SPIN	2P	193.17	174.83	B	B	12.50	173.08	6.70
MAXFLI XS 100	2P	192.83	172.17	A	B	12.37	171.80	6.47
DUNLOP DDH FOR WOMEN	2P	192.50	177.00	B	C	12.27	175.78	7.25
MAXFLI XD 90	2P	192.33	175.67	A	B	12.00	175.13	6.72
PRECEPT TOUR DOUBLE COVER	3PDC	192.33	172.50	A	B	12.17	172.28	6.63
SRIXON HI-BRID 3 PIECE	3P	192.17	174.17	B	C	11.60	173.35	6.65
TITLEIST PROFESSIONAL 90	3P	192.00	168.50	A	B	12.17	171.20	6.35
DUNLOP DDH 110	2P	191.83	175.67	B	B	12.17	174.20	7.03
WILSON STAFF TI DISTANCE 90	2P	191.67	177.33	A	A	11.96	175.25	6.88
MAXFLI XD 100	2P	190.83	176.83	B	B	12.00	175.08	6.73
GREG NORMAN SHARK SPIN	2P	190.83	174.17	B	C	11.96	172.97	6.62
WILSON STAFF TI BALATA 90	2PDC	190.83	171.83	B	B	12.50	172.55	6.40
RAM TOUR BALATA DC 90	2PDC	190.50	171.00	A	B	11.75	171.05	6.63
TITLEIST TOUR BALATA 90	3P	190.40	164.20	A	A	12.17	163.24	6.54
PRECEPT DYNAWING	2PDC	190.33	174.50	B	B	12.65	173.05	6.95
ULTRA 500 COMPETITION 90	2P	190.17	172.33	A	A	12.00	173.18	6.70
TOPFLITE STRATA TOUR 90	2PDC	190.17	171.33	A	B	12.00	171.50	6.45
TITLEIST HP-2 DISTANCE	2P	189.50	173.83	A	A	12.37	173.05	6.83
TITLEIST DT WOUND 90	3P	189.50	170.83	A	B	11.69	171.50	6.62
WILSON TC2 TOUR	2P	189.33	178.00	A	B	11.82	175.10	7.00

80 mph continued - **ALL BALLS TESTED WITHOUT PERFORMANCE GROUP RATING**

	Ball Type	Total Dist	Carry Dist	Carry Disp.	Total Disp.	Launch Angle	Ball Velocity	Traj.
RAM TOUR BALATA DC 100	2PDC	188.83	171.50	B	B	12.34	172.92	6.88
GREG NORMAN SHARK DISTANCE	2P	188.67	175.67	A	A	11.90	174.92	6.90
TOPFLITE STRATA ADVANCED 90	2PDC	188.67	172.83	B	B	12.00	172.67	6.63
MAXFLI HT BALATA 100	3P	187.00	165.50	A	B	12.34	169.00	5.97
RAM TOUR XDC 90	2P	186.50	170.33	B	B	11.20	171.75	6.82
RAM TOUR BALATA LB 100	2P	186.50	169.83	A	B	12.44	170.83	6.52
DUNLOP DDH CONTROL PLUS	2P	185.67	174.83	B	B	12.65	175.52	7.50
MAXFLI XF 100 DURABLE BALATA	3P	185.50	165.50	A	B	11.55	169.97	6.22
SRIXON HI-SPIN 2 PIECE	2P	185.33	170.17	B	B	12.10	172.40	7.13
MAXFLI HT BALATA 90	3P	185.00	162.50	A	C	11.80	167.38	5.85

90 MPH Swing Speed - Ranked by Distance

CLUB / SHAFT: OVERSIZED DRIVER, 10.5 DEGREE LOFT, REGULAR STEEL SHAFT

ALL BALLS TESTED WITHOUT PERFORMANCE GROUP RATING

	Ball Type	Total Dist	Carry Dist	Carry Disp.	Total Disp.	Launch Angle	Ball Velocity	Traj.
TOPFLITE XL 90 TITANIUM	2P	229.83	205.17	B	C	10.90	195.27	6.58
ULTRA 500 DISTANCE 90	2P	227.50	204.33	A	C	11.00	197.30	6.37
MAXFLI XD 100	2P	227.00	202.83	A	B	10.50	196.10	6.43
PRECEPT EV LADY	2P	226.50	205.33	B	C	10.50	195.13	6.47
TOPFLITE AERO	2P	226.33	201.00	B	B	10.60	193.47	6.55
MAXFLI XD 90	2P	225.33	201.83	B	B	10.60	196.22	6.58
PINNACLE EQUALIZER	2P	225.00	202.67	B	C	10.50	196.10	6.53
PRECEPT EV SENIOR	2P	224.83	203.67	B	B	10.40	195.00	6.50
MAXFLI XS 100	2P	224.83	198.00	C	C	10.30	192.57	6.28
TOPFLITE MAGNA DISTANCE 90	2P	224.50	202.50	A	A	10.24	195.17	6.58
PROSTAFF DISTANCE	2P	224.33	205.00	B	C	10.30	195.93	6.53
TOPFLITE HOT XL REG TRAJ	2P	224.17	202.83	B	B	10.30	194.90	6.37
GREG NORMAN SHARK DISTANCE	2P	223.83	205.83	B	C	10.55	196.48	6.75
TITLEIST DT 2 PIECE	2P	223.83	202.83	B	B	11.00	195.07	6.52
SLAZ 420P POWER CONTROL	2P	223.67	205.50	B	B	10.40	195.88	6.65
SLAZ 420T TOUR CALIBRE	2P	223.67	202.83	B	C	10.50	194.10	6.50
SLAZ 420D RAW DISTANCE PLUS	2P	223.33	204.83	A	B	10.60	195.97	6.82
TOPFLITE XL 90 PERFORMANCE	2P	222.83	201.67	B	C	10.45	193.85	6.37
UTLRA DPS ORIGINAL	2P	222.33	204.00	B	C	10.40	196.47	6.58
TITLEIST HP-2 DISTANCE	2P	222.33	203.00	A	C	10.34	194.35	6.78
DUNLOP DDH SPIN PLUS	2P	222.00	202.00	B	B	10.40	194.50	6.52
WILSON STAFF TI SPIN 90	2P	222.00	200.00	B	B	10.34	192.88	6.32
TOPFLITE STRATA TOUR 90	2PDC	222.00	198.50	A	B	10.24	192.15	6.22
PRECEPT TOUR DOUBLE COVER	3PDC	221.67	201.67	A	B	10.00	192.90	6.48
PROSTAFF PERFORMANCE SPIN	2P	221.67	200.33	A	B	10.80	194.07	6.32

90 mph continued - **ALL BALLS TESTED WITHOUT PERFORMANCE GROUP RATING**

	Ball Type	Total Dist	Carry Dist	Carry Disp.	Total Disp.	Launch Angle	Ball Velocity	Traj.
TITLEIST PROFESSIONAL 90	3P	221.67	195.17	A	B	10.30	192.93	6.13
DUNLOP DDH 110	2P	221.50	205.50	A	B	10.44	196.02	6.87
TOPFLITE HOT XL TOUR TRAJ	2P	221.50	205.00	B	C	10.55	195.40	6.62
DUNLOP DDH CONTROL PLUS	2P	221.50	205.00	B	B	10.60	198.22	7.15
TITLEIST DT WOUND 90	3P	221.33	199.83	A	B	10.80	193.63	6.45
GREG NORMAN SHARK SPIN	2P	221.17	201.83	B	C	10.50	194.35	6.33
WILSON TC2 TOUR	2P	221.00	206.50	B	C	11.14	196.38	6.73
DUNLOP DDH FOR WOMEN	2P	221.00	206.50	B	C	10.30	197.82	7.15
PRECEPT DYNAWING	2PDC	220.67	202.33	B	C	10.55	193.70	6.55
SRIXON HI-BRID 3 PIECE	3P	220.67	200.83	B	C	10.80	193.23	6.40
PRECEPT EV EXTRA DISTANCE	2P	220.33	205.50	A	B	10.80	195.28	6.82
PRECEPT EV EXTRA SPIN	2P	220.33	202.17	B	C	10.40	192.70	6.62
TITLEIST TOUR DISTANCE 90	3P	220.00	198.83	A	B	10.72	192.15	6.28
MAXFLI HT BALATA 100	3P	219.83	192.50	A	A	10.50	190.77	5.93
RAM TOUR BALATA LB 100	2P	219.50	197.83	B	C	10.30	190.88	6.32
ULTRA DPS TOUR SPIN	2P	219.33	201.33	B	C	10.30	194.05	6.27
RAM TOUR BALATA DC 100	2PDC	219.17	201.67	B	B	10.10	193.45	6.73
WILSON STAFF TI DISTANCE 90	2P	218.83	203.50	A	B	10.20	197.03	6.33
SRIXON HI-SPIN 2 PIECE	2P	218.67	200.67	A	B	10.30	192.77	6.75
RAM TOUR BALATA DC 90	2PDC	218.50	197.17	C	B	10.80	191.00	6.25
TOPFLITE STRATA ADVANCED 90	2PDC	217.83	201.67	B	C	10.00	193.63	6.37
TITLEIST TOUR BALATA 90	3P	217.40	193.60	A	B	10.30	187.54	6.50
MAXFLI HT BALATA 90	3P	216.50	189.00	B	B	10.50	188.43	5.88
ULTRA 500 COMPETITION 90	2P	216.33	200.00	B	C	10.30	193.95	6.33
MAXFLI XF 100 DURABLE BALATA	3P	216.17	192.00	A	C	10.30	190.25	5.85
RAM TOUR XDC 90	2P	216.00	200.33	B	B	10.50	192.08	6.58
WILSON STAFF TI BALATA 90	2PDC	215.50	197.00	B	C	10.60	193.15	6.08
TITLEIST HP-2 TOUR	2P	215.50	194.50	B	B	10.27	191.83	6.17

100 MPH Swing Speed - Ranked by Distance

CLUB / SHAFT: OVERSIZED DRIVER, 10.5 DEGREE LOFT, REGULAR STEEL SHAFT

ALL BALLS TESTED WITHOUT PERFORMANCE GROUP RATING

	Ball Type	Total Dist	Carry Dist	Carry Disp.	Total Disp.	Launch Angle	Ball Velocity	Traj.
TOPFLITE HOT XL REG TRAJ	2P	248.83	230.17	A	B	10.20	211.73	5.42
TOPFLITE HOT XL TOUR TRAJ	2P	246.50	230.83	B	C	9.60	212.20	5.77
SLAZ 420P POWER CONTROL	2P	246.50	230.33	D	D	9.60	212.72	5.75
PRECEPT EV EXTRA DISTANCE	2P	246.00	230.33	B	B	9.60	212.38	6.08
SLAZ 420D RAW DISTANCE PLUS	2P	245.83	230.50	B	B	9.20	212.75	5.83
WILSON TC2 TOUR	2P	245.83	230.33	B	C	8.85	213.47	6.25
TITLEIST TOUR BALATA 90	3P	245.80	220.60	B	B	9.30	206.58	7.00
WILSON STAFF TI DISTANCE 90	2P	245.50	230.50	B	B	9.50	214.22	5.93

89

100 mph continued - **ALL BALLS TESTED WITHOUT PERFORMANCE GROUP RATING**

	Ball Type	Total Dist	Carry Dist	Carry Disp.	Total Disp.	Launch Angle	Ball Velocity	Traj.
TOPFLITE XL 90 TITANIUM	2P	245.33	230.83	B	C	9.60	212.25	5.68
ULTRA 500 DISTANCE 90	2P	245.00	229.83	A	B	9.40	214.53	5.77
MAXFLI XD 90	2P	244.17	229.83	B	C	9.10	213.38	5.77
TITLEIST TOUR DISTANCE 90	2P	244.17	225.17	A	B	9.10	209.63	5.30
PRECEPT EV SENIOR	2P	244.00	228.50	B	B	9.90	212.25	5.75
PRECEPT EV LADY	2P	243.83	229.67	B	B	9.60	211.98	5.82
ULTRA DPS TOUR SPIN	2P	243.67	226.83	B	B	9.40	211.18	5.77
WILSON STAFF TI SPIN 90	2P	243.33	225.33	B	B	9.30	209.62	5.38
MAXFLI XD 100	2P	242.83	229.17	A	B	9.60	213.22	5.70
TITLEIST DT 2 PIECE	2P	242.83	228.83	A	A	9.60	212.28	5.45
TOPFLITE AERO	2P	242.83	226.67	B	B	9.75	209.95	5.67
PINNACLE EQUALIZER	2P	242.67	227.17	A	C	9.40	213.02	5.85
PROSTAFF DISTANCE	2P	242.33	229.17	A	B	9.30	213.55	5.85
TOPFLITE MAGNA DISTANCE 90	2P	241.67	227.33	A	B	9.50	212.12	5.70
UTLRA DPS ORIGINAL	2P	240.33	228.83	C	C	9.40	213.73	6.03
TOPFLITE STRATA ADVANCED 90	2PDC	240.33	226.50	A	A	9.10	210.93	5.80
TITLEIST DT WOUND 90	3P	240.33	225.33	A	B	10.80	209.85	5.65
TITLEIST HP-2 DISTANCE	2P	240.00	229.17	B	C	9.90	211.35	5.77
GREG NORMAN SHARK DISTANCE	2P	240.00	227.83	A	A	9.20	213.18	6.30
WILSON STAFF TI BALATA 90	2PDC	239.33	222.83	C	C	9.20	209.77	5.40
DUNLOP DDH CONTROL PLUS	2P	239.00	227.00	B	B	9.60	214.85	7.03
TITLEIST HP-2 TOUR	2P	238.50	220.83	A	B	9.30	208.27	5.38
TITLEIST PROFESSIONAL 90	3P	238.33	223.33	B	A	9.30	210.07	5.38
SLAZ 420T TOUR CALIBRE	2P	238.17	226.50	C	C	9.40	210.93	5.88
PRECEPT EV EXTRA SPIN	2P	238.17	223.00	B	B	9.10	209.65	6.18
PRECEPT TOUR DOUBLE COVER	3PDC	237.83	223.33	B	C	9.20	209.67	5.98
TOPFLITE XL 90 PERFORMANCE	2P	237.50	225.50	B	B	9.20	210.65	5.85
TOPFLITE STRATA TOUR 90	2PDC	237.33	222.50	B	C	9.10	208.67	5.33
RAM TOUR BALATA DC 100	2PDC	237.00	226.00	C	D	9.60	209.95	5.77
GREG NORMAN SHARK SPIN	2P	237.00	225.50	C	C	9.40	210.77	5.82
MAXFLI XS 100	2P	237.00	222.67	B	B	9.10	209.02	5.57
DUNLOP DDH 110	2P	236.83	227.83	C	C	9.40	212.37	6.62
PROSTAFF PERFORMANCE SPIN	2P	236.83	224.33	B	B	9.60	211.02	5.83
SRIXON HI-BRID 3 PIECE	3P	236.67	225.00	A	B	9.20	210.15	5.73
ULTRA 500 COMPETITION 90	2P	236.67	224.00	B	B	9.20	210.83	5.70
PRECEPT DYNAWING	2PDC	235.67	226.50	C	C	9.40	210.40	6.00
DUNLOP DDH SPIN PLUS	2P	235.00	225.83	C	D	9.20	211.20	6.02
MAXFLI HT BALATA 90	3P	234.50	216.83	B	B	9.10	205.23	5.03
RAM TOUR BALATA LB 100	3P	234.33	219.50	B	B	9.10	207.35	5.83
MAXFLI HT BALATA 100	3P	233.17	219.83	B	B	9.20	207.55	5.32
RAM TOUR BALATA DC 90	2PDC	232.50	219.00	C	C	9.30	207.17	5.70
RAM TOUR XDC 90	2P	232.33	221.33	C	C	9.40	208.63	6.00
DUNLOP DDH FOR WOMEN	2P	231.83	225.50	C	C	9.75	214.65	7.20
MAXFLI XF 100 DURABLE BALATA	3P	231.83	217.83	B	C	9.10	207.20	5.37
SRIXON HI-SPIN 2 PIECE	2P	230.33	223.83	C	B	9.20	209.78	6.17

Analyzing the Test Results

Distance - When analyzing *total carry* and *total distance* of each ball tested, on average, a two-piece ball carried farther than a three-piece ball at all swing speeds. Further analysis of *total distance* for each ball in all four performance groups showed a distinct pattern; golf balls in the performance group distance/durability contained the top performers in distance, especially at 90 mph and 100 mph swing speeds.

Velocity - In most cases, you will notice that the higher the *ball velocity*, the longer the carry and distance. *Ball velocity* is a key indicator in helping you determine which golf balls are hard or soft. The higher the *ball velocity*, the harder the ball. A hard ball will come off the face of the club faster, thus giving you a higher *ball velocity* rating. A softer ball, distinguished by either a soft cover and/or core, will come off the face of the club slower. When analyzing and comparing both *total carry* and *ball velocity* ratings of one ball over another, you may notice balls that have a higher *ball velocity* with a shorter *total carry* , while other balls having a lower *ball velocity* will have a longer *total carry*. A contributing factor to this type of results is the aerodynamics of the ball while in flight. Once a ball is in flight, the aerodynamics of the ball takes over with the help of it dimple pattern and spin rate. The results; the combination of the dimple pattern and spin rate of a ball could either help carry the ball farther (for a longer carry distance), or it can slow it down (for a shorter carry distance).

Dispersion - This is the accuracy rating of how straight the ball went. When analyzing this, look for how well the same ball performed for each test (i.e., the 80, 90 and 100 mph tests). First pick your club speed and your favorite ball. Now look at how well the ball is holding its accuracy in carry and distance (*carry dispersion* and *total dispersion*). Now check further the consistency of that same ball by looking at the *dispersion* ratings

of all three club speed tests. For example, let's say your ball had a *A/B* dispersion rating at the 80 mph test. Now check and see how sell that same ball did in the 90 and 100 mph test. Did it hold its accuracy?

90 versus 100 Compression - Based on our test results, there is little to no difference between a 90 and 100 compression ball of the same type. The average distance between the two types of balls was approximately two yards - either way.

Trajectory - We found that the trajectory differences on all of the balls tested in their swing speed category, even the balls that where labeled by the manufacturer as trajectory balls, were measured within the same one inch square increment. In some cases a low trajectory ball went higher than a high trajectory ball. If you're looking for a high or low trajectory ball, you may have better results toward solving your trajectory needs by using a club with a proper loft versus a ball type labeled as a high or low trajectory ball.

Competition - When ever you see an ad from a golf ball manufacturer showing their ball out performing all of the balls they're comparing too, look closely. Make sure the balls they're comparing too are balls of the same **performance group** as theirs. If you look at the test results of our independent testing, you will see a consistent performance pattern when comparing one performance group to another. For example, you will notice that a two-piece ball will almost always out perform a three-piece ball in distance. A harder ball typically always out performs a softer ball in distance. If their comparison is against balls from other performance groups, they're not comparing apples to apples -- or in golf terms, golf balls to golf balls.

Drivers

This section is an added bonus and a small sampling of what you can expect in future publications from StrictlyGolf. We decided to perform an independent test on a few of the most popular drivers on the market today and publish the test results. As with golf balls, you need to determine what clubs or driver fits your style of play. To help you, our independent study and test results will provide you with a better understanding of how a driver will perform.

But before we get into the test results, lets take a few minutes to better understand some of the newer driver technologies and how club manufacturers are trying to convince us to buy their driver. To help you wade through these claims and differences being made by the club makers, what follows is an attempt to help eliminate some of that confusion. We've also published results of our own independent study and tests of five of the most popular drivers on the market today. So read on because this section of the handbook may be your best golf partner and may even save you a few strokes and dollars before you purchase that driver.

Is It Real or Hype?

Golf is really like an obsession. If you think about it, it would be hard to pick a number big enough that some of us wouldn't spend if it would make us that much better.

As with golf balls, we can't help but feel perplexed every time we read or hear a manufacturers ad about their drivers. Every time anyone sees a new product, they think maybe it will make them a better player. The manufacturers love it, and they're feeding new designs and technologies at us faster than we can keep up. The industry that made the $300 titanium driver a commonplace, and not all that long ago, is now replacing it with the same but "improve" $500 titanium driver. And we're buying it!

We have such an ego problem when it comes to golf. Some golfers are really bad but still think they're Greg Norman, and what Greg uses, they'll use. If that club or ball works for him, its got to work for me! This is how the average golfer thinks. They're easily influenced and typically mimics someone else who is successful at using a particular club brand and model. As a result, a lot of golfers are buying a driver that they can't afford because they think they are buying a more enjoyable game. The game is addictive and the manufacturers know how to use it toward their advantage.

Those guys, the pros, the ones that are winning all of those tournaments using "your" driver, well, as good as they are, they probably can win with most any type of driver. They're being paid big bucks by the club manufacturer to use that driver in tournaments. A pro who has a contract with a club manufacturer is a walking billboard. That manufacturer owns his headgear, his bag and at least the front of his shirt. It's called "marketing!"

Every day the golf industry is seeing new youngsters and adults of all ages join the existing ranks of the more than 25 million golfers in the United States. This tremendous growth has shifted most golf club manufacturers toward investing more money in the research and development of equipment technology, manufacturing methods, and better merchandising techniques. As a result, they have us believing we need to upgrade to improve our game and we continue to buy their products.

The golf club industry is a multi-billion dollar industry that is introducing new products to us at a historic pace. We're seeing newer drivers and clubs being introduced almost every year by the same manufacturer with claims that it's either bigger and better or it's made with newer material and advanced technology. The fact is there's a golf club production war going on between the club manufacturers and they're all trying to determine how they can get an edge and keep it. Callaway is doing such a fine job at it that they have a factory which can produce a new set of clubs every five minutes, around the clock, just to keep up with the demand.

With the continuous advances being made in club technology, we're seeing more products and advertising claims being thrown at us from all angles and it continues to confuse both the professional and the average golfer.

To fully understand these claims, not only do we need a masters in physics and engineering, we need a tremendous amount of knowledge in club design. It may all sound and look good to us on paper, but once we hit the links it's a different story, one we wish we knew about before we invested another $500 to improve our game.

Todays Distance Drivers

Just what is behind all of these claims the club makers are telling us? When designing a driver, several components such as club head materials, aerodynamics, balance points and positioning, shaft, shaft weight and overall club length are significant factors toward providing increased distance in your drives. By understanding what role these factors play in your swing, it will help you find a driver that you'll feel comfortable with.

The Club Head

Titanium has been introduced by the club makers and is on the scene in full force. Almost all distance drivers feature titanium heads or titanium face inserts. The club makers love it because it's about 40% stronger and 20% lighter than stainless steel. Why distance with titanium? The truth is it's the weight and not the material that influences more distance. Titanium's light weight allows the club designers greater freedom to experiment with perimeter weighting, face depth and sole weighting in an attempt to create larger sweet spots to forgive the mishits. The problem though, with the adoption of titanium in the club head, you remove the weight from the club head thus taking away a certain amount of feel and control.

Controlling the Distance Driver

Because titanium is lighter, club makers are creating oversized club heads as big a 300cc's compared to the metalwood standard of 195cc's. However, the fact that titanium is allowing designers the ability to create oversized club heads doesn't necessarily make an oversized clubhead better. With an oversized clubhead there's more weight farther away from the hosel area causing difficulty for the average golfer to square the club face at impact. What typically happens is the toe of the club lags behind through the hitting area leaving the face open and sending shots off to the right (if you're swinging right handed).

What club makers are challenged with is to design an oversized driver that minimizes the club's resistance to squaring at impact while also lowering its center of gravity to help get the ball airborne. After all, what good is all that energy if you can't transfer it squarely to the golf ball? The distance driver's overall goal is light overall weight with substantial club head feel.

Another important factor toward achieving distance is the ultra-long shaft designs that are now available. In the days of the wooden club head, a 43.5" shaft was standard. Today, anything less than 45" is rare. Physics dictates that a longer shaft will generate more club head speed thus giving you more distance. The down side to this is the difficulty to control it. You need to experiment with this and find what is comfortable and easy to control.

Remember, there's really no secret in achieving more distance. If there is, it's making sure you hit the ball in the middle of the club face more often.

Drivers - Independent Test Results

The most thrilling shot in golf is the monstrous drive you just hit off the tee right down the middle of the fairway. At that very moment, no other shot can make you feel so good as does the one that not only lands smack in the middle of the fairway, but 30 yards past your playing partners. Club makers are doing and telling us everything they can to give you those extra yards and boost your ego.

But is that extra distance being promised by the club makers for real or is it hyped up marketing just to lure your attention and dollars?

StrictlyGolf performed an independent study and test on five of the most popular drivers on the market today and published our results. As with golf balls, you need to determine what clubs or driver fits your style of play. To help you, our independent study and test results will provide you with a better understanding of how a driver will perform.

Testing Criteria

The distance drivers used in our test were purchased from various off-course golf shops. An independent testing facility designed specifically for testing all outdoor golf equipment was used. Our drivers were tested under a controlled and wind free environment using proven testing methods to ensure consistency and quality results.

Using a custom built electro-mechanical hitting machine (a robot), performance data was collected for every driver tested. Each driver was tested at an 80, 90 and 100 mph swing speed.

For each driver tested, the same golf ball type and sample size was used. The golf ball type used in the test was a Titleist DT Wound 90. We performed center hits, toe hits and heel hits off each driver at all three swing speeds.

Distance Drivers Tested - Specification

Taylor Made Titanium Bubble 2

Loft: 10.5°
Lie: 58°
Length: 46"
Head Volume: 285cc
Swingweight: D6.5
Total Weight: 302
Shaft: Bubble 2 Shaft Graphite
Flex: Regular

Titleist 975D Titanium

Loft: 9.5°
Lie: 56°
Length: 45"
Head Volume: 260cc
Swingweight: D4
Total Weight: 330
Shaft: Ultralight Graphite
Flex: Regular
Shaft Weight: 65g
Flex Point: Mid

Callaway The Biggest Big Bertha Titanium

Loft: 10°
Lie: 56.5°
Length: 46"
Swingweight: D3
Total Weight: 292
Shaft: Ultra Light Graphite
Flex: Regular
Shaft Weight: 47 to 55g
Flex Point: Mid

Callaway Great Big Bertha Titanium

Loft:	10°
Lie:	56.5°
Length:	45"
Swingweight:	C9.5
Total Weight:	301
Shaft:	Ultra Light Graphite
Flex:	Regular
Shaft Weight:	47 to 55g
Flex Point:	Mid

Yonex Titanium Plus

Loft:	10.5°
Lie:	54½°
Length:	46"
Head Volume:	290cc
Swingweight:	E1
Total Weight:	277
Shaft:	Ultra Light Graphite
Flex:	Regular
Flex Point:	Mid

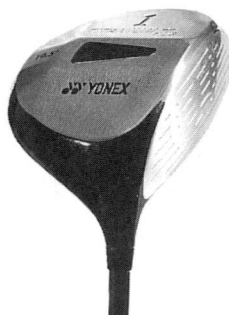

Driver Testing Parameters

Following are the definitions of the testing parameters used for the test. The same tests were performed for each driver at 80, 90 and 100 mph swing speeds.

Drivers Tested

- Taylor Made Titanium Bubble 2
- Titleist 975D Titanium
- Callaway The Biggest Big Bertha Titanium
- Callaway Great Big Bertha Titanium
- Yonex Titanium Plus

Ball Type Used for Test

For each driver tested, the same golf ball type and sample size was used. A Titleist DT 90 Wound three-piece construction golf ball was used.

Driver Loft

The loft angle of the club as given by the manufacturer.

Launch Angle

Measured in degrees, this is the initial launch angle of the ball off the club head at that speed.

Total Carry

Measured in yards, the total distance of the ball while in flight.

Total Distance

Measured in yards, the total distance of the ball's carry and roll.

Carry and Total Dispersion

This ranking represents the accuracy of how straight the ball stayed on target for total carry and total distance. This is a measurement that is either left or right from a centerline that is perpendicular from where the ball is launched.

Ball Velocity

At the point of impact of the ball leaving the club head, the speed of the ball in feet per second.

80 MPH Swing Speed - Driver Test
GOLF BALL USED: TITLEIST DT 90 WOUND

DRIVER	Loft	Launch Angle	Carry Disp.	Carry Dist.	Total Disp.	Total Dist.	Ball Velocity
Taylor Made Titanium Bubble 2	10.5	11.60					
Center Hits			5.25	167.88	6.25	193.38	173.41
1/2" Toe Hits			4.50	162.13	10.63	186.75	171.15
1/2" Heel Hits			5.38	159.88	7.13	185.75	170.11
Titleist 975D Titanium	9.5	11.10					
Center Hits			2.31	169.50	3.81	191.63	173.25
1/2" Toe Hits			6.91	165.00	8.78	188.50	171.26
1/2" Heel Hits			16.00	163.75	13.00	186.50	168.99
Callaway Biggest Big Bertha Ti	10	10.20					
Center Hits			2.34	169.89	5.78	193.63	175.58
1/2" Toe Hits			18.38	165.88	20.00	190.13	173.65
1/2" Heel Hits			25.00	162.50	29.13	186.85	170.98
Callaway Great Big Bertha Ti	10	10.30					
Center Hits			2.50	169.25	8.25	185.88	174.44
1/2" Toe Hits			24.38	167.13	33.13	188.13	171.66
1/2" Heel Hits			25.13	162.13	25.88	184.93	168.93
Yonex Titanium Plus	10.5	9.50					
Center Hits			3.25	162.88	8.25	189.50	174.96
1/2" Toe Hits			15.50	155.38	21.25	185.00	173.23
1/2" Heel Hits			9.25	160.88	9.88	187.50	172.73

90 MPH Swing Speed - Driver Test
GOLF BALL USED: TITLEIST DT 90 WOUND

DRIVER	Loft	Launch Angle	Carry Disp.	Carry Dist.	Total Disp.	Total Dist.	Ball Velocity
Taylor Made Titanium Bubble 2	10.5	10.00					
Center Hits			4.38	198.88	5.88	218.38	192.58
1/2" Toe Hits			6.25	190.50	9.38	215.36	189.74
1/2" Heel Hits			7.50	194.13	10.88	213.50	191.15
Titleist 975D Titanium	9.5	9.60					
Center Hits			3.09	194.50	4.31	219.38	193.71
1/2" Toe Hits			11.84	192.75	14.59	217.75	191.85
1/2" Heel Hits			8.94	187.13	11.34	206.63	188.85

continued - 90 MPH SWING SPEED - DRIVER TEST

Callaway Biggest Big Bertha Ti	10	10.40					
Center Hits			2.47	201.25	3.78	224.63	193.95
1/2" Toe Hits			16.38	197.50	21.75	217.88	192.24
1/2" Heel Hits			8.91	192.00	7.13	212.75	187.60
Callaway Great Big Bertha Ti	10	9.60					
Center Hits			5.88	196.50	7.50	211.63	192.04
1/2" Toe Hits			11.25	194.50	11.88	207.13	187.00
1/2" Heel Hits			18.38	191.13	22.25	210.13	186.24
Yonex Titanium Plus	10.5	8.10					
Center Hits			2.50	191.38	6.88	220.88	196.06
1/2" Toe Hits			16.25	185.63	19.75	215.63	193.05
1/2" Heel Hits			8.00	187.50	11.75	210.50	192.75

100 MPH Swing Speed - Driver Test
GOLF BALL USED: TITLEIST DT 90 WOUND

DRIVER	Loft	Launch Angle	Carry Disp.	Carry Dist.	Total Disp.	Total Dist.	Ball Velocity
Taylor Made Titanium Bubble 2	10.5	9.60					
Center Hits			5.78	230.88	10.19	257.25	215.93
1/2" Toe Hits			8.19	227.00	11.81	249.13	213.01
1/2" Heel Hits			5.31	222.63	8.03	246.13	211.13
Titleist 975D Titanium	9.5	7.40					
Center Hits			3.06	226.13	5.38	244.00	215.08
1/2" Toe Hits			12.75	226.50	15.88	241.00	214.41
1/2" Heel Hits			12.50	220.00	12.00	236.88	209.89
Callaway Biggest Big Bertha Ti	10	8.60					
Center Hits			6.38	232.63	8.47	254.88	218.20
1/2" Toe Hits			5.09	230.00	6.47	254.25	216.34
1/2" Heel Hits			41.38	223.75	40.88	245.88	212.59
Callaway Great Big Bertha Ti	10	9.20					
Center Hits			3.25	232.63	55.31	246.88	216.56
1/2" Toe Hits			16.13	226.25	18.69	239.38	213.89
1/2" Heel Hits			16.56	222.75	18.31	234.00	211.81
Yonex Titanium Plus	10.5	7.30					
Center Hits			5.38	228.25	7.47	251.50	220.00
1/2" Toe Hits			18.25	222.75	19.38	246.63	216.80
1/2" Heel Hits			21.47	226.13	29.09	250.63	215.85

Analyzing the Test Results

Total Distance on Center Hits - The following drivers performed the best when measuring *total distance* for each swing speed:

80 MPH Swing
- Callaway's The Biggest Big Bertha Titanium at 193.63 yards.

90 MPH Swing
- Callaway's The Biggest Big Bertha Titanium at 224.63 yards.

100 MPH Swing
- Taylor Made Titanium Bubble 2 at 257.25 yards.

Center Hit Accuracy - The following drivers performed the best when measuring center hit accuracy for each swing speed:

80 MPH Swing
- The Titleist 975D Titanium with a total dispersion of 3.81 feet.

90 MPH Swing
- The Callaway's The Biggest Big Bertha Titanium with a total dispersion of 3.78 feet.
- The Titleist 975D Titanium in a close 2nd with a total dispersion of 4.31 feet.

100 MPH Swing
- The Titleist 975D Titanium with a total dispersion of 5.38 feet.

Drop Off In Carry Distance - Drop off In Carry Distance against Center Hits with Toe/Heel Hits. The following are the drivers which lost the least amount of *total carry yardage on toe/heel hits* when compared to *total carry yardage on center hits*. This measurement is an indicator of which driver recovers best when a mis-hit, or

off-center hit occurs. This measurement also helps indicate how weight disbursement of the driver effects mis-hits.

80 MPH Swing
- The Callaway's Great Big Bertha Titanium. 2.12' lost on toe hit, 7.125' lost on heel hit.

90 MPH Swing
- The Callaway's Great Big Bertha Titanium. 2.00' lost on toe hit, 5.42' lost on heel hit.

100 MPH Swing
- The Titleist 975D Titanium. .37' gained on toe hit, 6.13' lost on heel hit.

Interestingly enough, the Yonex Titanium Plus was a close 2nd in recovering from off center mis-hits at all speeds. It out performed all drivers in heel hits.

Glossary

Address The position taken by a golfer when preparing to start a swing or stroke.

Approach A shot from off the green aimed at getting close to the pin (hole).

Backspin The reverse spin imparted to a ball by the clubhead making the ball fly higher and farther, and stop quicker on the green.

Balata Natural or synthetic compound used to make the cover for high-quality golf balls. Its soft, elastic qualities produce a high spin rate, and it is favored by tournament players.

Ball mark The indentation in the turf made when a lofted shot lands on the putting green.

Compression Today, golf ball compression refers to the feel of the golf ball. There are typically two types of compression ratings for golf balls; low compression and high compression. At impact, a low compression golf ball actually flattens against the club face giving you more impact time of the ball on the club head with more feel. A high compression ball is harder and leaves the club head quicker upon impact. The compression rating is usually imprinted on the ball; 90 for low compression, 100 for high compression. If the compression rating is not imprinted on the ball, black lettering with a black number on the ball depicts high compression and black lettering with a red number on the ball depicts low compression. A faster club head speed will flatten the ball more than a slower speed when hit, no matter what the ball's compression.

Core The core refers to the material used inside the golf ball.

Core, Solid A two-piece ball consists of a solid core and a durable cover. While the basic composition of high performance two-piece golf ball cores are a common Polybutadiene (PBD), there are considerable differences in specific formulation and size. Some golf balls have larger core sizes than others which contributes to a softer feel.

Core, Wound

A wound or three-piece golf ball consists of the center, the windings and the cover. The center is either solid or hollow-filled. The cover is typically balata or Surlyn. The center is generally made of a rubber compound. Most balata covered golf balls feature a hollow center that is filled with either a liquid or paste material. The type of center in combination with the windings and cover material affect the spin rate and feel of the ball.

Cover

The important characteristics of golf ball covers is flexibility which is affected by thickness, hardness and material type. These three characteristics when combined together can create the reflexive qualities of the golf ball cover which attributes to a softer feel, optimum spin and better playability. The covers of most golf balls used by the weekend golfer are durable plastics made of a blend of synthetic polymers.

Dimples

Dimples are tiny depressions on the golf ball that allows for accuracy and distance when the ball is in flight. You will find that each manufacturer may have differently designed dimple patterns on their golf balls which helps control the type of flight path of the ball. The best performance pattern isn't based on the total number of dimples or geometric design, but rather a combination of all the variables involved. Aerodynamics and testing have proven that it isn't only dimples, but also the patterns they're arranged in, that make the golf ball soar.

Dimples, Deep

Dimples that are deep generate less spin than shallow dimples, which decrease lift and cause the ball to stay on a low trajectory, with less air time and greater roll.

Dimples, Large

Large dimples generally give the ball a higher trajectory and longer flight time.

Dimple Pattern, Atti/Octahedral

The most common pattern for many years was the atti, which is four straight rows of dimples around the middle of the ball, four around each pole (top and bottom), with small triangular arrays of dimples filling the leftover space. This crisscrossing of rows creates four large triangular dimple groupings on each half of the golf ball, eight in all, so the pattern in call octahedral. Balls with this pattern generally have low trajectories.

Dimple Pattern, Deltahedral This pattern is very similar to the icosahedral pattern but has 24 triangular groups of dimples. The deltahedral pattern is also called Tetraicosahedral by MacGregor who uses this pattern on their balls.

Dimple Pattern, Dodecahedral This pattern contain any triangles but arranges the dimples into 12 pentagonal arrays. The theory is that the pentagon provides more possibilities for repeating patterns. These patterns are used by Dunlop DDH balls.

Dimple Pattern, Icosahedral This pattern was introduced in the early 70's and is the most popular design. The dimples are divided into 20 triangular groups, and as the ball spins, it consistently presents the same dimple pattern to the air it encounters, cutting down air resistance.

Dimple Pattern, Tetrahedron This dimple pattern is in the shape of triangles. The tetrahedron pattern consists of four triangles.

Dimples, Shallow Shallow dimples generate more spin on a golf ball than deep dimples, which increase lift and causes the ball to rise and stay in the air longer and roll less.

Dimples, Small Small dimples generally give the ball a lower trajectory and good control in the wind.

Draw A shot that is controlled to make the golf ball go from right to left.

Driver Spin Shows the balance between distance and workability. Less spin denotes longer, straighter distance, more spin equals more shot-making control.

Elastomer A proprietary cover material that Titleist is using that is said to surpass the current industry standards of balata and surlyn. It's a material that is designed to provide the best of both worlds -feel and durability.

Fade A shot that is controlled to make the golf ball go from left to right.

Feathery An early golf ball made by filling a leather pouch with boiled feathers. It was highly susceptible to damage and began to go out of use in the mid-1880s after the introduction of the cheaper guttie ball.

Feel Indicates how soft or firm a golf ball will feel to the golfer off the club face, especially on and around the greens.

Guttie Ball introduced in 1848, made of gutta percha, a rubber-like substance obtained from the latex of a species of Malaysian rubber trees.

Lie Angle This is the measurement between the hosel and the ground. It strongly influences a shot's direction. The correct lie angle will give you a straight shot from a square hit. If the angle is too upright, the heel of the club will dig too deeply and the ball will start left of your target (if right handed shot). If the lie angle is too flat, the toe will dig in, causing the ball to start right of your target.

Loft Although each club has a specific loft, it is affected by club head speed, swing path, and the angle of the approach. As a rule of thumb, more loft is better than too little because extra loft creates additional backspin, which in turn, reduces sidespin. This is more important to woods than irons because you usually have a wider choice of wood lofts.

Rubber-core Ball The golf ball, invented by Coburn Haskell in 1898, that revolutionized the game at the turn of the century. Also known as the Haskell ball, it was composed of a solid rubber center around which was wound many yards of elastic thread under tension. It was then covered in gutta percha. The rubber-core ball superseded the guttie.

110

Shaft Flex Shaft flex is primarily based on swing speed and tempo. The proper shaft for a player's club head speed results in the club head rotating correctly so it is square to the target at impact. If the shaft is too shift the club head will lag behind, thus reducing loft and causing the ball to fly lower and to the right. If the shaft is too weak for a player's swing, the club head will overtake the shaft at impact causing high shots that go to the left.

Spin Rate The amount of spin on a golf ball. The spin rate affects a player's ability to work or "control" a golf ball. A high spinning golf ball tends to carry longer, roll less, and reacts more to side spin which allows a golfer to intentionally draw or fade the ball. Most manufacturers of golf balls provide extensive testing to identify the optimum amount of spin for their balls. They have found that golf balls imparting too much spin sacrificed performance and distance, while golf balls imparting too little spin sacrificed control. You will find that most manufacturers will provide competitive two-piece high performance golf balls that rate from very high spin rates (which could result in lack of distance and susceptible to up-shooting in windy conditions) to low spin rates (which could sacrifice control and workability).

Swingweight This defines the distribution of weight throughout a club. Some players prefer the feel of a light swingweight (C8 to D0 for men), where relatively more weight is toward the grip end. Other players may prefer heavy swingweights (D7 to E1), where relatively more of the club's total weight is toward the head.

Surlyn Is the most widely used cover material. This material is called an ionomer which is a thermoplastic resin. The most commonly used ionomer, Surlyn, is a trademark for the resin developed by the Dupont Company nearly twenty years ago. This material is more durable than balata, offering better cut and abrasion resistance. Surlyn is chemically different than balata, so while offering improved durability, Surlyn covered golf balls generally feel harder than balata balls and are less flexible which results in low spin rates. But since its introduction, many advancements have been made to improve the performance of Surlyn and its feel.

Trajectory High trajectory golf balls are balls that are designed for a higher flight and long distance. A high trajectory ball is usually designed to spin more on club impact and flight. Low trajectory golf balls are balls that are designed for improved accuracy in the wind and increased iron distance and the flight pattern is typically lower with extra roll. A low trajectory ball is usually designed to spin less on club impact and flight. Speed, spin and dimples determine the trajectory of a ball.

Velocity In terms of golf balls, the initial velocity refers to distance.

X-Outs These are golf balls that have a row of X's stamped over the brand name. These balls usually are first-quality balls that were rejected for cosmetic defects such as bad inking of the printing on the ball. However, some companies sell X-Outs that are balls with slightly off centered cores or inexact compression's.

Zylin A cover material that is used by Spalding for their Top-Flite balls. It's a material that is designed to provide feel and durability.

Companies Who Make Golf Balls

Golf ball manufacturers welcome the consumer to inquire about their products. This list of manufacturers was compiled so that if you need to inquire about additional information or statistics on their golf balls you can either write to them or call their consumer relations department.

Acushnet/Titleist
P.O. Box 965
Fairhaven, MA 02719-0965
800-225-8500
www.titleist.com

Cayman Golf Co.
P.O. Box 5287
Albany, GA 31706
800-344-0220

Ram Golf
Hansberger Precision Golf
238 Industrial Circle
Pontotoc, MS 38863
800-647-8122
www.ramtour.com

Wilson Sporting Goods Co.
8700 West Bryn Mawr Ave.
Chicago, IL 60631
800-622-0444
www.wilsonsports.com

Ben Hogan Company
8000 Villa Park Drive
Richmond, VA 23228
Customer Service:
800-631-9000

David Geoffrey & Associates
Slazenger
P.O. Box 7259
Greenville, SC 29611
800-766-2615
www.slazengergolf.com

Spalding Sports Worldwide
425 Meadow Street
P.O. Box 901
Chicopee, MA 01021-0901
800-642-5004/800-443-3776
www.topflite.com

Bridgstone Sports (USA), Inc.
15320 Industrial Park Blvd. NE
Covington, Georgia 30209
800-358-6319
www.preceptgolf.com

Dunlop Golf Division (Maxfli)
P.O. Box 3070
Greenville, SC 29602
800-476-5400
www.dunlopsports.com

Srixon
Sumitomo Rubber Industries
Distributed by Tad Moore Golf, Inc.
LaGrange, Georgia 30240
www.srixon.com